Guide to the…

Wekiva River Basin State Parks

By Don Philpott
Wekiva Wilderness Trust

Table of Contents

Foreword

I have been very fortunate in my life to travel to many exotic and wonderful places but few can rival the natural beauty of the Wekiva River Basin State Parks. It is even more remarkable that in the heart of the world's top tourist destination - which attracts over 40 million visitors a year - there is this wonderful, pristine oasis.

Hike one of the trails in one of the parks and you could be a thousand miles from the glitter and razzmatazz of Disney World, Universal Studios and the other world-famous attractions. Stand on the deck outside the nature center at Wekiwa Springs and look out at a view that has changed little over thousands of years.

The basin state parks are special for many reasons. They have a rich and fascinating history. They boast more habitats than any of the other Florida state parks and have, therefore, a more diverse flora and fauna. They provide an invaluable wildlife preserve in one of the state's major metropolitan areas. They provide a wealth of recreational opportunities and they contain one of the nation's most beautiful rivers.

I have been a regular visitor to the parks for 15 years and have volunteered for the last ten. I've had the opportunity to work on many projects and events including helping to staff the nature center and do guided walks and interpretive programs.

This book is an attempt to help answer many of the questions that have been asked by visitors to the nature center and for which I had no answer. In researching and writing this guide I have learnt so much about the parks' fascinating history, their habitats, their wildlife and above all, how important it is that we all do everything we can to protect them.

For me this has been a labor of love. My hope is that you enjoy reading about our wonderful basin parks as much as I have enjoyed writing about them. Please enjoy them and support them.

That support is needed more now than ever before. Water quality and quantity of our rivers and springs is a major concern and soon the Wekiva Parkway will cut across a corner of park land. We don' t know what other issues will arise in the years ahead but we must all do everything we can to protect and preserve our parks.

Note: If you have any interesting information about the basin parks and their history or have any old postcards or photographs of the parks, I would love to hear from you so that we can add to future editions of the guide. You can send information to me at:

Wekiva Wilderness Trust
1800 Wekiwa Circle
Apopka FL 32779

The Author:

Don Philpott has spent almost 50 years traveling the world, first as a journalist and then as a travel writer and expeditioner. He co-founded Footloose, an environmental outdoor activities magazine in his native Britain. He relocated his marketing and public relations firm to Florida in 1988 and is now a full-time writer and volunteer. He has written more than 140 books, many about Florida, the Caribbean and the great outdoors. He has had a lifetime passion for wildlife, both photographing and watching it and has backpacked, climbed, canoed, ridden and skied throughout Europe, North America, Africa, Asia, the Arctic, Australia and New Zealand. He is an instructor with the University of Florida's Master Naturalist Program and a member of the National Association for Interpretation and the National Press Club.

Acknowledgements

I would like to thank all those who assisted me and supported me while researching and writing this book. A lot of the information in this book has been taken from public records and public domain sources such as Websites and publications of the Florida Department of the Environment, Florida Fish and Wildlife Conservation Commission, Florida Division of Recreation and Parks and the St. Johns River Water Management District.

My special thanks go to Warren Poplin, manager of the Wekiva River Basin State Parks, Anne James, former Park Services Specialist (PSS) and Scott Mowry, the current PSS, and Paul Lammardo, park biologist. Double thanks go to Paul and Christy Burch, former assistant manager, for their artistic illustrations.

Thanks also to Dick Ashby for his encouragement and diligent editing and Harry Rodis, for his encyclopedic geophysical knowledge – and for being a long-standing stalwart of the Wekiva Wilderness Trust. Finally, my thanks to all members of the WWT and our volunteers for the tremendous work they do.

While the publishers and author have used their best efforts in preparing this book, they make no representations or warranties with respect to the accuracy or completeness of the contents of this book.

Published by Wekiva Wilderness Trust
1800 Wekiwa Circle
Apopka FL 32712
www.wwt-cso.com
info@wwt-cso.com

FLORIDA STATE SYMBOLS

State Flower – *Orange Blossom*

State Bird – *Northern Mockingbird*

State Mammal – *Florida Panther*

State Tree – *Sabal Palm*

State Shell – *Horse Conch*

State Marine Mammal – *West Indian Manatee*

State Freshwater Fish – *Largemouth Bass*

State Saltwater Fish – *Sailfish*

Introduction to the Parks

Wekiwa Springs State Park (WSSP), Rock Springs Run State Reserve (RSRSR), and Lower Wekiva River Preserve State Park (LWRPSP) – collectively known as the Wekiva River Basin State Parks (WRBSP) – are located in Lake, Orange, and Seminole Counties, approximately 20 miles northwest of Orlando.

The Wekiva Basin ecosystem is an outstanding natural resource: the Wekiva River and its tributaries have been designated an Outstanding Florida Water, a National Wild and Scenic River, a Florida Wild and Scenic River, and a Florida Aquatic Preserve.

The parks contain 40,952 acres - Wekiwa Springs State Park 9,441 acres, Rock Springs Run State Reserve 13,994 acres and Lower Wekiva River Preserve State Park 17,517 acres.

Wekiwa is a Creek Indian word for "bubbling" or "boiling" water, and today the crystal clear spring attract visitors year round. Wekiva is the Creek word for "running water" and is the name of the river that is fed by the springs. Much of the river corridor is Hydric Hammock, Floodplain Swamp and Floodplain Marsh.

The Wekiva River Basin State Parks are important not only because they area a magnificent natural oasis in a rapidly developing urban area, but because they display 19 distinct natural habitats, more than any other state park in Florida.

Wekiwa Springs State Park

Wekiwa Springs is one of the gems in the Florida State Parks system. If you stand on the deck outside the nature center, you can enjoy a panorama that has changed little over the centuries. The landscape, vegetation and wildlife are much the same as when the first Indians arrived almost 12,000 years ago and even when the first Spanish explorers ventured inland almost 500 years ago.

The main spring vent is 15 feet below water level and discharges nearly 43 million gallons of clear water a day and the lagoon, which is about 20 feet deep, has a temperature that remains between 68 and 72 degrees year round.

There are 26 known springs in the Wekiva River Basin, being part of the more than 700 springs in Florida, the largest collection of freshwater springs on earth. First magnitude springs discharge more than 65 million gallons of water a day.

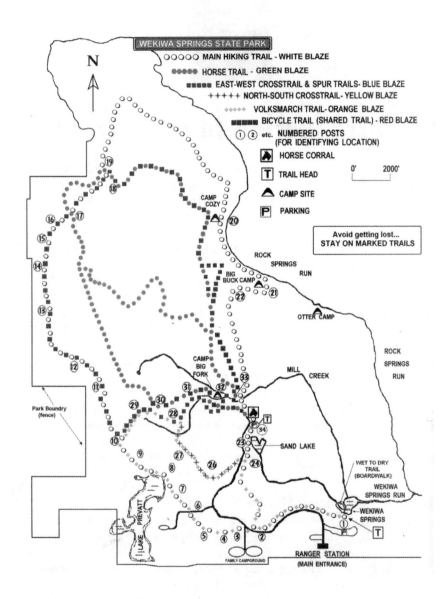

WEKIWA SPRINGS STATE PARK

N

OOOOO MAIN HIKING TRAIL - WHITE BLAZE
●●●●● HORSE TRAIL - GREEN BLAZE
■■■■■ EAST-WEST CROSSTRAIL & SPUR TRAILS- BLUE BLAZE
+++++ NORTH-SOUTH CROSSTRAIL- YELLOW BLAZE
◇◇◇◇◇ VOLKSMARCH TRAIL- ORANGE BLAZE
▨▨▨▨▨ BICYCLE TRAIL (SHARED TRAIL) - RED BLAZE
① ② etc. NUMBERED POSTS (FOR IDENTIFYING LOCATION)

🔥 HORSE CORRAL
T TRAIL HEAD
▲ CAMP SITE
P PARKING

0'   2000'

Avoid getting lost...
STAY ON MARKED TRAILS

CAMP COZY

⑲
⑱
⑯ ⑰
⑮
⑭
⑬
⑫
⑪
⑩
⑨
⑧
⑦
⑥
⑤ ④ ③ ②
①

⑳

ROCK SPRINGS RUN

BIG BUCK CAMP
㉒ ㉑
OTTER CAMP

ROCK SPRINGS RUN

CAMP BIG FORK
㉝
㉜
㉛
㉚ ㉙
㉘
㉗ ㉖ ㉔ ㉓

MILL CREEK

㉞
㉓
SAND LAKE

Park Boundry (fence)

WET TO DRY TRAIL (BOARDWALK)
WEKIWA SPRINGS RUN
WEKIWA SPRINGS
T

LAKE PREVATT

FAMILY CAMPGROUND

RANGER STATION
(MAIN ENTRANCE)

Wekiwa Springs is a second magnitude spring – classified as any spring discharging between 6.4 and 64.6 million gallons a day. Wekiwa Springs State Park now covers almost 9,500 acres and the springs form the headwaters of the 15-mile long Wekiva River. This flows into the St. Johns River which flows north to Jacksonville and then discharges into the Atlantic Ocean.

The park is home to 73 designated species of plants and animals that are listed as endangered, threatened or of special concern. There are 19 different plant communities found within the park providing year-round food and protective cover for a diverse and abundant animal population from Florida black bears to gopher tortoises and Sherman's fox squirrels to the rare Limpkin.

A total of 163 bird species have been recorded in the park although two birds that used to live in the park – the ivory-billed woodpecker and the dusky seaside sparrow – are now extinct. The former disappeared because its habitat was destroyed and the latter became extinct because of the number of people in the area.

In the 19th century it was said that there were so many manatees in the Wekiva River that it was hard to maneuver. Salt water shells and sharks teeth have been found in the area between the parking lot and Wekiwa Springs Road, a reminder that all this area was under water in the distant past.

Interpretive Pavilion

The nature center, next to the concession area but soon to move to a more prominent location, gives an overview of the natural history of Wekiwa Springs State Park and the Wekiva River Basin. We encourage you to learn more about the rich diversity of flora and fauna, some of which is threatened and endangered.

The Wekiwa Springs Nature Center is sponsored by the Wekiva Wilderness Trust (WWT) and staffed by volunteers. The WWT is a citizens' support organization dedicated to the preservation and restoration of the natural environment and promotion of nature-related activities within the Wekiva Basin. The organization is made up totally of volunteers and is dependent on contributions for financial support. WWT receives no local, state or federal financial support.

How to get here:
Access the park by heading west on State Road 434 from Interstate 4 (Exit 94). Heading north on Wekiwa Springs Road from State Road 434, the park entrance is on the right.

Rock Springs Run State Reserve

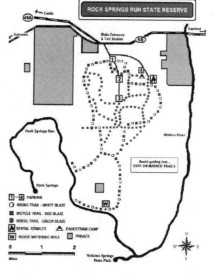

Rock Springs Run State Reserve covers just over 14,000 acres of diverse habitats and plant communities – 13,698 acres of upland and 312 acres submerged. It was purchased in 1983 with funds from the Conservation and Recreation Lands (CARL) Program for habitat protection and opened as a park in 1984. The reserve borders more than 12 miles of the Wekiva River and Rock Springs Run

There are many Indian mounds and "kitchen middens" as a reminder of some of the area's first inhabitants. A unique feature of the reserve is that it is almost ringed by the spring-fed river system - ideal for canoeing - and rich in wildlife. There are several trails. The Buffalo Tram Trail is an old railroad bed used by the logging companies to haul cypress out.

How to get here: Access the reserve by exiting Interstate 4 at State Road 46 (Exit 101C) and proceeding west for seven miles. The park entrance is on the south side of State Road 46.

Lower Wekiva River Preserve State Park

The Lower Wekiva River Preserve State Park covers more than 17,500 acres (13,796 upland acres and 3,721 acres submerged) and borders about six miles of the St. Johns River and the lower four miles of the Wekiva River and Blackwater Creek. It opened in 1977 but land acquisitions since have significantly expanded the park and created a natural wildlife corridor along the Wekiva and St. Johns Rivers extending into the Ocala National Forest. A special feature of the preserve is the system of blackwater streams and their associated wetlands which provide habitats for a number of rare and endangered species.

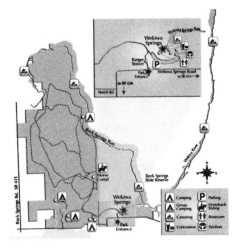

How to get here: The park is northeast of Rock Springs Run State Reserve and is located within Seminole and Lake Counties. The eastern entrance can be reached by exiting Interstate 4 at State Road 46, Exit 101C and proceeding west 4.2 miles. The entrance is on the north side of State Road 46. The northern entrance is off State Road 44 in Pine Lakes.

Economic Importance
The Florida state park system has an overall direct economic impact of over $1 billion on local economies throughout the state. Direct economic impact is defined as the amount of new dollars spent in the local economy by non-local park visitors and by park operations. Over $65 million is contributed to general revenues in the form of state sales taxes. In addition, over 18,700 jobs are generated as a result of the state parks' operations.

The implication of this data is that for every 1,000 people attending a state park, the total direct impact on the local community is over $43,200. On average, if a state park were closed for one year, it would mean a loss of nearly $5.9 million to the local economy. If the state park system increased its annual attendance by 10 percent, it would impact the state's economy by an additional $65 million. Volunteers contribute more than 1.2 million hours each year to the Florida Park Service. The Wekiva River Basin State Parks attract more than 265,000 visitors a yea. They spend almost $11.5 million in the local area, creating a direct economic impact of almost $12.5 million.

FUN FACTS
Did You Know?

When a **black bear** rears up on its hind legs, it isn't being threatening. It just wants to get a better look at you.

Alligators continue to grow teeth throughout their lives.

Gopher tortoises can live up to 100 years.

Many **grasshoppers** and crickets have their ears on their front legs.

A good way to determine the length of a submerged **'gator** is to estimate the distance in inches between the eyes and the tip of the nose and multiply this by feet. If the eye to nose is about 10 inches, then you are looking at a 10-foot gator.

Alligators can out-swim you in the water and outrun you on land - achieving speeds of 35 mph over short distances. Large gators can also jump four to five feet vertically out of the water.

Florida **black bears** do not usually hibernate, but some Florida **spiders** do.

Dragonflies are sometimes referred to as Florida Mosquito Hawks because their favorite food is the pesky mosquito.

An **osprey** can be traveling at 50 mph when it hits the water in its feet-first dive for prey.

The **rhinoceros beetle** can carry 850 times its own weight on its back.

A **tick** can live up to five years without feeding.

Geology and Hydrology

Central Florida is composed mostly of sand overlying several hundred feet of porous limestone. The limestone, also known as the Florida Aquifer, is cavernous and stores rainwater that percolates down from the surface to constantly recharge it. The Florida Aquifer is the largest underground body of fresh water in the world. By the time the rainwater reaches the aquifer it is slightly acidic and reacts with the limestone to sculpt it enlarging the fissures and cracks into caves. In places, the caverns and void spaces collapse giving rise to sinkholes and lakes.

The whole area is underlain by rock formations formed over millions of years and several geological times. The uppermost and youngest formation is exposed at the surface and was formed during the Pleistocene period. It consists largely of unconsolidated sand, gravel, silts, clays and peat. Underlying the Pleistocene deposits is the Miocene layer, the next oldest, and made up mostly of limestone. It includes the Chipola, Hawthorn, Chatahoochee and St. Marks Formations.

Underlying this layer and formed during the Oligocene period are the Suwannee and Marianna Formations and below that are the older Ocala limestones, also formed during the Oligocene period. The Aquifer formed during Eocene times and consists of limestone and dolomite that is older than the middle Miocene period and younger than the early Eocene period – the oldest.

Fossils dating back 17 million years have been found at Rock Springs. The variety in topography and soil types within the parks contributes to the diversity of hydrologic regimes.

The flow of springs in the Wekiva Basin is influenced by geologic and hydrologic factors. These are 1) the interconnecting caverns and porous spaces extending from spring vents into the aquifer and 2) pressure head differences between the spring vent and the higher recharge or replenishment areas. Today spring flow is decreasing and water quality diminishing because of increased pumping from wells that tap the aquifer and by polluted surface water that replenishes the aquifer.

History

Whon dinosaurs roamed the rest of North America, Florida was still submerged several hundred feet below the sea. Instead of massive land animals, the warm waters above what was to become Florida were home to giant sharks - more than 55 feet long - whales and giant dugong, related to today's endangered manatee.

After Florida emerged from the sea between 40 and 25 million years ago, North America was affected by the ice age. So much water was trapped in the glaciers that the levels of the Atlantic Ocean and Gulf of Mexico were much lower – as much as 350 feet lower than today – and the peninsula was twice the size of modern day Florida. It obviously had a much cooler climate and there were few flowing rivers and wetlands. At this time mammoth, mastodons, saber tooth tigers, camels, rhinoceroses, giant ground sloth, giant beavers, wolves and glyptodonts (a 1,000 lb ancestors of the armadillo) roamed the countryside. All had been driven south by advancing Ice Age glaciers. The oldest items found in Wekiwa Springs are pieces of fossilized ivory dating back to around 10,000 years ago although artifacts dating to 12,000 BC have been found near Lake Apopka.

PaleoIndians

Around 11000 BC Paleo-Indians arrived in Florida. Their ancestors had entered North America from eastern Asia across a huge land bridge exposed by the lower sea levels. They were wandering hunters and gatherers although they rarely hunted big game. Their diet consisted mainly of small animals, plants, nuts and shellfish. Because there were few rivers, their settle-

ments were built close to springs, sinkholes and water holes where animals also had to come to drink. The northern glaciers started retreating about 8,500 BC and Florida's climate became warmer and wetter as the sea level rose.

This encouraged more people to migrate south and establish settlements in other areas. It was around this time that the Paleo-Indian culture evolved into the

Middens and Shell Mounds

A midden is effectively a settlement's garbage tip that over the years grows in size until it becomes a mound. Once the settlement is abandoned the midden gets covered with vegetation. This flora is unique due to the high ph of the calcium shells. A professional exploration can reveal enormous information about the lives of the people. Midden deposits can contain animal bone, shells, botanical material, pottery fragments and other artifacts that can tell how people lived and what they ate. Middens with damp conditions can even preserve organic remains that can yield information about climate and seasonal use.

There are many middens and shell mounds in the parks although many of them are of undetermined age and many have been vandalized and damaged.

Some of the more notable middens are:

- Haystack Midden, a dome shaped St. Johns midden on the north side of Rock Springs Run.
- Rollins Island, a large St. Johns 1 shell midden on the eastern shores of the Wekiva River.
- Love's Cabin, a shell midden at the north end of Rock Springs Run. It gets its name because the shack was built by trapper Clyde Love. It was built in the 1930s and removed in 1981.
- Big Buck Hunting Camp, a St. Johns shell midden on the south side of Rock Springs Run.
- Katie's Landing, a large shell mound on the north end of the Wekiva River, past State Road 46.
- Pennel's Cabin is a St. Johns shell midden on the south shore of the junction of the Wekiva River and the Little Wekiva River. A cabin, now removed, used to stand on top of the midden.
- Pappy's Cabin is a small St. Johns shell midden on an island east of Twin Mounds. The cabin that was built on the midden has long since been removed.
- Twin Mounds- adjacent shell and snail middens – on the west bank of the Wekiva River that are on the National Register.

Early Archaic culture that saw the first permanent settlements. The Indians were skilled weavers and twine makers using fibers from Sabal palm, saw palmetto and other plants. The twine was used to weave cloth, make fish nets and rope. Tools and weapons were made from bone.

The Early Archaic culture evolved into the Middle Archaic culture around 5,000 BC. People established villages along wetlands and near rivers and their locations were so favorable that they flourished generation after generation.

Around 3,000BC, Florida's climate was much the same as it is today and the Late Archaic period began. This was the time when the largest shell maddens accumulated as shellfish and fish were a major food source. The people lived in large villages and learned how to fire pottery, tempering it with Spanish moss and palmetto fibers. By about 500 BC the Archaic culture, dominant throughout Florida, began to fragment into regional cultures. Each developed its own distinctive pottery which has helped archaeologists identify and study specific cultures. One of these cultures was the St. Johns – named after the river along which they lived. These Timucuans were farmers and fishermen and their settlements have been found throughout the region. Spear heads and pottery shards have been found in the springs and Wekiva riverbed and at least six early campsites have been documented along the Wekiva River and Rock Springs Run. Spear heads are often mistaken for arrow heads but bows and arrows had not been introduced then. Most spear heads and knives were made from chert not flint. Chert is formed by the precipitation of silica to form nodules and is the most common material used in Florida for points.

Indian pottery shards dating back to 2,500 BC have been found. Of more recent origin are finds of flints and ivory used for spearheads although these are at least 1,500 years old as Indians didn't start using bows and arrows until about 500 A.D. There are 50 known archaeological sites with the boundaries of the Parks and Native Americans lived around Wekiwa Springs, Rock Springs and the Wekiva River throughout the Pre-Columbian period, beginning with the PaleoIndians and continuing through the Archaic, Mount Taylor, Orange, Transitional and St. Johns Periods.

Amerindian Timeline
Paleo-Indian period — 12,000 B.C.
Archaic period — 6,000 B.C. – 1,000 B.C.
Mount Taylor period — 4,000 B.C. – 2,000 B.C.,
St. Johns period — 500 B.C.-A.D.1565

The Paleo-Indians lived in villages of 25 to 30 houses. Each home was round and about 25 feet in diameter. In the winter the roof was made of thatched palms and in the hot summer, reeds were used that allowed the air to circulate.

Primarily hunters and gatherers, they did plant crops such as maize, beans and squash, including pumpkins. They made tools and artifacts from bone, stone and shells. They used fiber from the cabbage palm to make ropes and fishing nets and for weaving cloth.

They used dugout canoes, made from pine or cypress. The shallow, narrow canoes were up to 20 feet long and had a platform at each end for poling the boat or fishing. When on long trips, they would often sink their canoes and cover them in mud so that they were protected until they returned for them. Many of their shell middens are located along the banks of the Wekiva River, Rock Springs Run, and Wekiwa Springs.

The Spanish

In the 1500s the first Spanish explorers arrived. Apart from horses and oranges, they brought with them European diseases that killed most of the Indians. In 1513 there were six or seven main groups of Indians throughout Florida with about 40,000 Timucuans in Central Florida.

In the 1700s, Seminole Indians, descendants of the Creek Indians, moved into central Florida from Alabama and Georgia, taking over the areas formerly inhabited by the Timucuans. The origin of the word Seminole is not certain. Some say it is derived from a Creek word meaning "runaway" – someone who has left the main camp and settled elsewhere – while others argue it "comes from 'cimarron', a colloquial Spanish word for "wild".

The English

In 1763 Britain gained control of Florida from the Spanish by exchanging it for Havana, Cuba, which they had captured during the Seven Years War. The British tried to populate the area by offering land and in July, 1768 Scottish doctor Andrew Turnbull arrived with 1,400 indentured workers and settled at New Smyrna creating the biggest settlement in Central Florida. The settlement collapsed after a few years and the people moved north to St. Augustine. British rule ended in 1784 as part of the Treaty of Paris that concluded the American Revolution. Florida was returned to Spain.

Exploration

In 1774 William Bartram, the first botanist to explore southeastern North America, made camp near the Wekiva River. He recorded the plants and animals of the area. The Seminoles helped him explore and named him Puc Puggy or "flower lover".

Settlement and Seminole Wars

In the late 18th and early 19th century settlers began colonizing Central Florida and by the mid-1800s, the area was primarily used for farming and milling. As more settlers moved into Florida there was increasing conflict as they took over Seminole lands. The First Seminole War (1817-1818) took place and in July, 1821 the United States formally took control of Florida. Pressure grew on the U.S. government to remove the Seminoles from Florida and this led to the Second Seminole War (1835-1842). The only battle of the Seminole Wars in Orange County was fought in the swamps of Wekiva on July 29, 1840. The enemy killed Private Isaac Childs of the Second Regiment of Dragoons on that day. After the war, many Seminoles were exiled to Creek reservations west of the Mississippi. Many refused to leave their lands and a few hundred escaped south into the Everglades.

Statehood

On March 3, 1845 Florida became the 27th state of the United States of America. Almost half its population was made up of enslaved African Americans working on cotton and sugar plantations. Peter Buchan with his family and slaves established the first plantation close to the springs in the 1840s.

The Third Seminole War broke out in 1855 – again because white settlers wanted to take over Seminole lands. The war lasted three years and at the end of it there were estimated to be less than 100 Seminoles left in Florida.

In 1860 Florida's population was only 140,424 and almost half were slaves. Most of the population was in the northern part of the state. Central Florida was largely uninhabited.

Early Tourism

At the end of the Civil War, Florida started to become a popular tourist destination. A hotel was built at the springs and tourists started arriving to enjoy the year round good weather and the warm waters of the springs.

Wekiwa Springs, then known as Clay Springs after farmer L. H. Clay, was a popular destination, not only for Orlando and area residents but also for people from up and down the St. Johns River. Clay Springs was also the name of the community that had sprung up along the Wekiva River. It had about 100 residents and was important as it served as port and shipping point for the Apopka-Zellwood area. Barges brought in food and supplies to the warehouse and dock at Clay Springs and would then take oranges and lumber to the St. Johns River, where steamboats carried it to Jacksonville. The township had a saw mill, printing shop and factory where oranges were pressed into wine. After the big freeze, the orange packing house was turned into a skating rink and attracted folks from miles around – and on Sundays it doubled as the church. Joel D. Smith was the town postmaster - appointed by President Grover Cleveland – and mail was brought up river from Mellonville, the original name for Sanford,

The hotel at the springs, attracted tourists who traveled in and out by wagon or took the river steamers for the 28 mile trip from the Port of Sanford on the shore of Lake Monroe. Sanford was also the terminus of the South Florida Railroad and in 1880 the Sanford to Orlando rail extension was opened. In 1888 President Grover Cleveland and his wife visited Sanford to support tourism in the state.

Wekiwa Hotel

The Wekiwa hotel was built by a Mr. J. A. Smith who established a township called Sulphur Springs. He also changed the name of the springs to 'Sulphur Springs' although the name didn't catch on and the locals still referred to it as Clay Springs.

From the 1880s to 1890s, in addition to the hotel, tourism facilities included a sanitarium, cabins, bathhouse, boat docks, and a rail toboggan ride down the slope into the springs. Clay Springs also boasted a newspaper and five two-storey homes.

It is said that when families picnicked at the springs, the men always brought along their Winchester .44 rifles because wild pigs were such a problem in the nearby woods.

River Transport

Some time in the mid to late 19th century a ferry boat that transported people across the Wekiva River sank. It is now a shipwreck site within the boundaries of Wekiwa Springs State Park. The first steamboat operating on the Wekiva River was built by Capt. T. W. Lund and his father and went into service in December 1874. It operated from Clay Springs to the mouth of the Wekiva connecting with steamers from Jacksonville. In 1877 Capt. E. R. Laws announced he would make two trips a week between Sanford and Clay Springs in the Mayflower, a 70-foot double ended vessel with a 14-foot beam, a sidewheel and a draft of only 14 inches.

Henry Sanford's store in Sanford also opened a branch in Clay Springs and did considerable business with local farmers. He supplied merchandise on credit to those who consigned their cotton crops to him.

In 1887, Amos Schultz from Norristown, Pennsylvania, a winter resident of Clay Springs, opened the Clay Springs Wine Company making wine from oranges. He had 15 employees and planned on making 2,000 barrels of wine a year. While he never reached his target, the company did make wine until the mid-1890s.

Around 1890 the springs were operated as a picnic ground by the Steinmitz brothers. There were rowing boats and a large naphtha launch used for sightseeing trips down the river. At 4 pm every day, a large flock of wild turkeys would swoop down on to the bluff west of the spring where a generous supply of corn was laid out for them.

In 1894 a sanitarium and 100-room hotel opened at the springs. It was owned and operated by Dr. C. L. Randall from Chicago. He called it Toy-Y-A-Watha believed to have been the Native American name for "healing waters."

The doors opened on November 1st and rates ran from $1.50 a day to $6 a week. Water from the spring was said to help ailments from rheumatism to arthritis and was bottled and sold. Wekiwa Springs can lay claim to being Florida's first amusement park as it had a tram ride into the springs and a dance pavilion.

The town's prosperity was built on the surrounding fruit growing areas but was dealt a mortal blow by the great freeze of 1894-95. With no fruit to ship, the people moved away and the township disappeared although the springs continued to attract visitors. The old sanitarium and hotel were destroyed by fire in the early 1940s.

Early 20th Century

A second smaller hotel was built in the early 1900s by the Wekiwa Springs Company and boasted indoor plumbing and poolroom.

The name Clay Springs was changed in 1906 to Wekiwa Springs, and ever since there has been confusion about the names Wekiwa and Wekiva.

In the early 1920s a tour boat sailed between Wekiwa Springs and the St. Johns River and the river was still used to bring in supplies and mail to areas such as Zellwood and Winter Park.

In 1923 Detroit entrepreneur M. E. Miller bought Wekiwa Springs and opened a real estate office. He cut three streets, laid miles of sidewalk and started to promote Wekiwa as "a wonder spot". Two years later he reopened the Wekiwa Springs Hotel and sold one lot. At the end the 1920s, with only two lots sold, he gave up and nature reclaimed the streets and sidewalks.

In 1935 the Wilson Cypress Co. built a narrow gauge railway into the swamp to haul out the centuries-old cypress trees. The Florida Park Service was created the same year.

The town of Markham, located south of Lake Markham, operated from around 1880 to 1945. Pinnie Ridge Cemetery, also known as Pinnie Grove Cemetery, is thought to contain between 24 and 75 burial sites, but no headstones or cemetery markers remain.

African-American Links

Plantation House and Mitchell Farm House is an African-American historic site consisting of the remains of some agricultural buildings and a refuse pile.

Another historic African-American site south of Lake Markham is where the Oak Grove Missionary Baptist Church stood. It was built in the mid-1880s and is reported to have burned down in 1928.

Ethel is an historic cemetery, reported to have been the community cemetery for the railroad stop town of Ethel, formerly called Moody. There were a number of saw mills in the area and there was a spur line from Ethel to the mills. Located east of County Road 433, it is currently the oldest known cemetery in Lake County. Four grave markers remain intact.

Logging and collecting turpentine were other important industries in the area

Turpentine

The turpentine industry moved into the area in a big way in the 1880s and 1890s to provide rosin and oil (or spirit) of turpentine for naval stores. Rosin was used to caulk the ship's timbers to make them watertight. A turpentine farmer would typically have about 10,000 trees. He needed workers to "crop" them, quarters for them to live in and a still to convert the gum.

During the winter the trees were "boxed" which involved attaching a box or cup to a tree about 10 inches from its base. A V- shaped deep cut was made above the cup. In the spring the sap started to rise and would flow from the cut into the cup.

Every few days, a worker would return to make another cut just above the old one to keep the sap running. This continued for eight to nine months. The series of cuts was called a "face". Every few weeks, the cup would be emptied into buckets which would then be emptied into barrels and taken by cart to the still.

The huge copper stills were heated until the gum boiled. The liquid was passed through a coil and collected in a tank. As it cooled the oil of turpentine rose to the surface and was drained off into barrels. The rosin left in the still was filtered and then packed into barrels or seven gallon hurdy pots where it congealed before being sent to market.

The best crop was always in the first year that trees were tapped. The yield dropped off each successive year. A good crop would be about 50 barrels of turpentine and 160 barrels of rosin.

Turpentine trees could be tapped for between three and five years and then be allowed to rest for a year or two before the cycle started again. They could only be tapped a few times because once faces had been cut around the tree no more sap could be drawn.

until the 1940s. On very old pines you may still spot the incisions cut into the bark to extract the turpentine. There are many logging trails throughout the basin parks.

One of them, the Logging Trail, was built in the early 1940s in the St. Johns River flood plain cypress swamp. A segment can be followed across Banana River and out to Bush Island. The site consists of a pilings constructed from local woods with some retaining metal spikes. In 1941, the Apopka Sportsmen's Club purchased the property from the Wilson Cypress Company and it was maintained for recreational use.

The Silver Screen

In the 1950s, the Wekiva River became a popular backdrop for several motion pictures, including Yellowneck (1955), The Girl from 5,000AD (1957) and Johnny Tiger (1966).

Hunting Club

The Apopka Sportsmen's Club maintained the area for recreational use until they sold it to the Florida Park Service in 1969. A memorial to the Club members can be seen at Sand Lake.

Wekiwa Springs State Park

On April 30, 1969, the Board of Trustees of the Internal Improvement Trust Fund obtained title to the property that later became Wekiwa Springs State Park. The park opened July 1st 1970. In its first year, it attracted more than 300,000 visitors. In 1971 the park was so popular that officials imposed a 1,000 person limit at any one time and added a 25c admission charge.

Rock Springs

The first settler at the springs was thought to be W. S. Delk, who came from Georgia who moved to Florida in the 1840s. Ox carts brought in supplies from Hawkinsville, 18 miles away on the St. Johns River. At that time Orlando was a small trading post, the only one between Jacksonville and Tampa.

The first house was a log cabin just north of the springs. The house burned down when Delk tried to burn out the fleas from underneath it. The next house was built on the hill on the south side.

Trees were cleared and the land was planted with cotton, sugar cane and rice.

He built a dam across the stream about 50 yards from the spring and a flume with a big bucket water wheel in it. The dam was on the right hand side as you look down the stream. The spillway was on the left and next to the waterwheel was a grist mill, were saw mill and cotton gin that were operating by 1861. By 1863, he

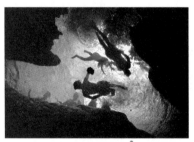

owned nearly 3,000 acres of land and was the largest planter in the area. Delk died in 1885 aged 70.

Over the years the basin parks have been expanded with the acquisition of more land. Today the parks are almost 40,000 acres of natural vegetation, habitat and wildlife - little changed from when the first Indians arrived thousands of years ago.

The Springs
of the Wekiva River Basin

The Florida Aquifer covers almost 82,000 sq. miles underlying all of Florida plus parts of neighboring Alabama, Georgia and South Carolina. In parts of Central Florida the aquifer – often called Florida's rain barrel - is more than 2,000 feet thick. Rainwater percolates down through the sand and is trapped in the limestone below. The water then bubbles back up to the surface or well drilled to bring the water to the surface.

Geologists estimate that there are more than 700 springs in the state of Florida, representing perhaps the largest concentration of freshwater springs on earth. Their outflow ranges from less than a gallon a minute to 1.3 billion gallons a day at Spring Creek Springs in Wakulla County. Florida has 27 of the nation's 78 first-magnitude springs (each discharging 64.6 million gallons or more a day or 747 gallons a second) – more than any other state. Florida also has about 70 second-magnitude springs (each discharging between 6.46 and 64.6 million gallons a day). All the spring water comes from the aquifer. The pressure of water rising vertically from a large spring creates ripples on the surface that is known as a "boil". Salt water underlies the fresh water aquifer throughout Florida.

The Wekiva Basin Area includes the aquifer ground water and the recharge areas or "springshed" including surface waters. There are 31 known springs in the Wekiva River Basin. These springs form the base flow for many of the rivers in the basin and create a unique and productive ecosystem.

The Wekiva River is a spring-fed system associated with 19 springs connected to the Floridan Aquifer. Of these, 11 are second and third magnitude springs.

According to a recent study by the University of Florida Water Institute (Summary and Synthesis of the Available Literature on the Effects of Nutrients on Spring Organisms and Systems, 28 April 2008), it is known that:

- *Springs and spring runs represent a unique class of aquatic*

ecosystems typified by high water clarity, relatively constant water temperature and chemical conditions, and complex biotic interactions.

- *In their natural state, springs persist in a quasi environmental steady-state* and due to this stability have developed complex biological systems that are highly efficient at converting solar energy into useful productive work.

- *During the past century humans have been exerting an increasing variety of external and internal stresses on spring ecosystems in Florida,* the most pervasive include:

  - Alteration of discharge regimes resulting from increased groundwater withdrawals

  - Increased levels of nutrients, particularly nitrate-N in groundwaters discharging from springs

  - Extensive recreational disturbance of springs and spring runs

  - Increased disturbance in the form of management actions, for instance exotic species control.

Ecosystem Implications of Invasive Aquatic Plants and Aquatic Plant Control in Florida Springs

- *Major problems with nonnative plants in Florida began with the introduction of water hyacinth, into the St. Johns River in the late 19th century.* Water hyacinth was documented in several springs ecosystem along the St. Johns River by the mid 1890s.

  Chemical control programs have maintained water hyacinth populations at low levels throughout Florida since the mid-1970s.

- *Historical sightings by William Bartram indicate that water lettuce, a floating aquatic plant, has been present in a number of Florida springs since at least 1765.* Scientists disagree as to whether water lettuce was present in Florida before European colonization, or was introduced by early Spanish settlers. Chemical control programs have maintained water lettuce at low levels throughout Florida since the mid-1970s.

- *Hydrilla became established in several areas of Florida, including the Kings Bay/Crystal River springs complex, by 1960.* Sustained control of hydrilla, a submersed aquatic plant, has proven more difficult than the floating plants in Florida. Most aquatic plant management costs in Florida springs ecosystems over 2005 – 2006 were associated with chemical control of hydrilla.

- *Observations from several springs suggest a "boom-bust" successional sequence in which nonnative plants first out-compete native plant communities, and then suffer catastrophic population crashes associated with aquatic plant control or natural disturbances.* Succession of springs into algal-dominated ecosystem states may be promoted by the nutrient pulses and ecological openings associated with the rapid loss of aquatic plant populations.

- *Water hyacinth and water lettuce emit allelopathic compounds capable of suppressing a number of algal taxa.* The effects of such allelopathic compounds on algal dynamics in springs' ecosystem are not presently known.

- *Ecosystem surveys indicate that water hyacinth, water lettuce, and hydrilla provide attractive habitat for crayfish, apple snails, amphipods, fish, manatees, and other springs fauna at moderate levels of coverage.*

- *Observational accounts suggest that aquatic plant control activities may sometimes have significant adverse effects on springs' fauna.* Depression of dissolved oxygen due to decaying biomass is a primary concern to animals following aquatic plant control. Copper and diquat herbicides also pose concerns in terms of direct toxicity to some animals at levels used for aquatic plant control.

- *Water hyacinth and water lettuce are currently being managed for algal-suppression, nutrient recovery, and biomass utilization in a number of tropical countries, including places in which they are considered nonnative.* Careful experimentation with similar ecosystem recovery methods may be worthwhile in highly degraded springs ecosystems where these plants are established.

- *Biotypes of hydrilla that are resistant to fluridone, a systemic herbicide commonly used for hydrilla control in Florida lakes, have been documented in recent years.* Thus, there is increased concern about the potential evolution of hydrilla strains that are resistant to Aquathol®, the contact herbicide most commonly used to control hydrilla in springs.

- *Establishment of selective biological control organisms is increasingly viewed as a priority for sustainable control of hydrilla in Florida.* A potential biological control for hydrilla, the hydrilla tip mining midge (*Cricotopus lebetis*), has been documented in Kings Bay/Crystal River, and may be suitable for experimental introduction into other springs systems.

Sinkholes

Sinkholes are part of the natural erosion of limestone which is soluble in water. Florida gets between 48 and 60 inches of precipitation a year on average and as this rainfall percolates through the limestone layers it washes away particles of rock and creates cracks which over millions of years develop into huge caverns holding water. If the dissolving limestone roof of the cave is just below the topsoil, it collapses and creates a sinkhole, called a collapse sinkhole. This is a natural process and these collapses occur throughout the limestone layer, often several hundred feet underground. A sinkhole that developed in Winter Park in May, 1981 was about 350 feet in diameter.

Wekiwa Springs forms the largest spring pool in Wekiwa Springs State Park. At an elevation of approximately 25 feet above sea level, the springs form the headwaters of the 17-mile long Wekiva River, a tributary of the St. Johns River. The springs are located at the base of a grassy hillside used by park visitors for picnicking and recreation. The spring pool is kidney-shaped, and it measures 105 feet in diameter. The main vent/fissure is situated in an east-west orientation in the southeastern portion of the pool. It is a 35 foot long fissure in exposed limestone. Average depth over this vent is 13.7 feet. The secondary vent is located 100 feet to the east-northeast of the main vent, and it is approximately two feet high and 15 feet wide.

Combined average discharge from these two boils is approximately 43 million gallons per day, or almost 68 cubic feet per second. The spring responds to rainfall with relatively small and delayed increases in discharge. The spring bottom is sandy and averages 5 feet deep. A sidewalk and small retaining wall with access steps for swimmers encompass the springs, and a wooden footbridge is located 200 feet downstream from the main pool. Although the Wekiva River supports a diverse plant community, the diversity of aquatic vegetation in the springs is limited and biomass fluctuates seasonally. From the spring pool, water flows northeast in a run approximately 60 feet wide. Floodplain Swamp and Hydric Hammock border the run. The spring-run flows for approximately one-half mile before it intersects with Rock Springs Run, and these two spring runs form the Wekiva River.

Other Springs

Witherington Spring, one of several springs found on the unit. Witherington Spring is a third magnitude spring with more than one pool. Its largest boil is about 60 feet in diameter and has an average discharge of 3.81 cubic feet per second.

Sulfur Spring is located on the Kitteridge Tract. Some hydrological restoration was done on this spring in 2001 to restore the spring to its original condition and prevent further erosion at the site. The pool is oval in shape (20 feet by 40 feet) with clean, clear water flowing out from a sand boil about five feet in diameter. Depth in the spring ranges from several inches at the outflow to approximately 12 feet deep at the boil. The water has a strong sulfurous odor.

Island Spring is a submerged spring located in the middle of the Wekiva River just north of the State Route 46 Bridge. This spring vent has been surveyed to a depth of 65 feet. Beyond 65 feet the spring is no longer penetrable to divers. The main vent slopes down from the river bottom through sand, silt, and clay layers to a depth of 30 feet where a vertical shaft then continues through the fossilized dolostone to the bottom. Flow in this system is coming from two areas: vertical flow emanates from the bottom and lateral flow enters from a side vent located at 30 feet of depth. Average discharge from this system is nine cubic feet per second. Water flowing out of this spring has a very high salt concentration (presumably from an ancient connate deposit), and populations of mullet (*Mugill cephalus*) and blue crab (*Callinectes sapidus*) are seen frequenting the vent.

Nova Spring is a submerged spring located in a slough to the eastern side of the main channel just north of the State Route 46 Bridge. The spring has a large sand boil with clear flowing water emerging at about 15 feet of depth. Anecdotal accounts suggest that the spring is man-made, but that has not yet been verified.

Barrel Spring is located just north of the main park drive in a low seepage area approximately 0.75 miles west of Wekiwa Springs. Although named Barrel Spring, it is actually a seep.

Main Spring Name	Magnitude	Discharges
SEMINOLE COUNTY		
Sanlando	2	Little Wekiva River
Starbuck (Sheppard) Spring	2	Little Wekiva River
Palm Spring	3	Little Wekiva River
Miami Spring	3	Wekiva River
Harden Spring	Unexamined	Wekiva River
ORANGE COUNTY		
Rock Springs	2	Wekiva River via Rock Springs Run
Wekiwa Springs	2	Wekiva River via Wekiwa Springs Run
Witherington Springs	3	Wekiva River via Rock Springs Run
LAKE COUNTY		
Island Spring	3	Wekiva River
Barrel Spring	Unexamined	Wekiva River
Messant Spring	2	Wekiva River via Seminole Creek
Seminole Springs	2	Wekiva River via Seminole Creek
Camp La No Che Spring	2	Wekiva River via Blackwater Creek
Moccasin Spring	Unexamined	Wekiva River via BlackwaterCreek via Seminole Creek
Palm Spring	Unexamined	Wekiva River via Blackwater Creek via Seminole Creek
Droty (Drody) Spring	Unexamined	Wekiva River via Blackwater Creek via Seminole Creek
Sulfur Spring	Unexamined	Wekiva River via Blackwater Creek via Sulfur Run
Sharks Tooth Spring	Unexamined	Wekiva River via Blackwater Creek via Sulfur Run
Unnamed Springs	Unexamined	Wekiva River via Blackwater Creek via Sulfur Run (.5 mi. E of Sharks Tooth Spring)

Wekiwa Springs & the Floridan Aquifer

Surficial Deposits
Largely unconsolidated and mostly permeable sand, silt, clay, peat and carbonate deposits.

Confining Beds of less permeable silt, clay and clastics overlay the Floridan Aquifer.

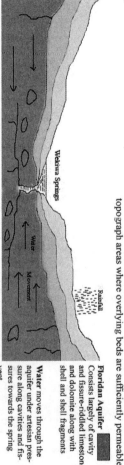

Rainfall recharges the Floridan Aquifer generally in higher topograph areas where overlying beds are sufficiently permeable.

Floridan Aquifer
Consists largely of cavity and fissure-riddled limestone and dolomite along with shell and shell fragments

Water moves through the aquifer under artesian pressure along cavities and fissures towards the spring vent.

Wekiwa Springs

Water

Movement

Rainfall

Geological cross section of the Wekiwa Basin (not to scale) showing Wekiwa Springs and related features

Springs discharge and vent

Wekiwa Springs discharges about 43 million gallons per day from several caverns and fissures in the aquifer. The largest spring is at the southwest part of the pool where the vent is about five feet wide and 15 feet below the pool surface. Spring discharge is measured at a gaging station at the footbridge below the pool. **Note:** The combined discharge of springs in the Wekiva Basin is about equal to that used by the City of Orlando for municipal supply.

Water Quality & Temperature

Selected water quality constituents in milligrams per liter are:

Total dissolved solids	190
Sulfate	20
Chloride	15
Nitrate & Nitrite	1.5
Orthophosphate	0.10

Temperature at the vent is about 74°F year-round.

Geologic age of strata shown in the above cross section.

Surficial deposits	} Holocene and Pleistocene	
	10,000-900,000 years ago	
Confining Beds	} Upper Miocene	
	5-10 million years ago	
Floridan Aquifer	} Miocene, and Eocene	
	10-45 million years ago	

Wekiva River Drainage

The Wekiwa Springs are the headwater of the Wekiva River which flows northeast 14.4 miles to join the St. Johns River. Several other springs in the Basin also contribute to the Wekiva River.

Note: Spring discharge and water quality data from USGS and SJRWMD.

The Wekiva River

The Wekiva River begins at the confluence of the Wekiwa Springs Run and Rock Springs Run and runs for 16 miles to join the St. Johns River. Along the way two tributaries run into it – the Little Wekiva River and Blackwater Creek. The watershed covers about 130 square miles with elevations above sea level ranging from 15 feet to 195 feet.

The Wekiva River is important because of the biological communities in its basin, the purity of its water – mostly spring-fed – and the archaeological objects that have been found along its banks.

Several springs contribute to the Wekiva River accounting for the high flow volume and the relatively steep drop in the river. It drops about 1.6 feet per mile over its course, making it one of the steepest rivers in Florida.

The Wekiva River Basin

The Wekiva River Basin is located in a region of biological transition between two climatic zones, where the range of temperate zone plants overlaps the northern limit of some tropical species which produces a wide diversity of species.

Over 20 species of threatened plants have been listed, including many ferns and orchids, as well as many wildlife species.

The Wekiva River is one of the few remaining near-pristine riverine systems in central Florida. Its headwaters begin at the confluence of Wekiwa Springs Run and Rock Springs Run.

The Wekiva is a major tributary of the St. Johns River. Waters forming the upper reaches of the Wekiva River arise from both the Floridan aquifer in the form of clear, natural springs and from drainage of approximately 130 miles of watershed.

The Little Wekiva River and Blackwater Creek are two major tributaries of the Wekiva. Blackwater Creek, which begins at Lake Dorr in the Ocala National Forest, drains an additional 126 square miles of watershed into the lower reaches of the Wekiva, just upstream of the St. Johns River.

An extensive floodplain of hardwood forest is approximately three miles wide in some areas. The Lower Wekiva River starts at Lake Lawne in the Pine Hills area and runs north through canals and underground pipes until it emerges above ground again about 13 miles south of its confluence with the Wekiva River.

Wekiva River Aquatic Preserve

The Wekiva River Aquatic Preserve was established by the Florida Legislature on June 23, 1975 through the Florida Aquatic Preserve Act (Chapter 258.35-258.45, Florida Statutes). In June 1985, the Legislature passed Senate Bill 762, which expanded the boundary of the Wekiva River Aquatic Preserve to include approximately 20 miles of the St. Johns River.

The Wekiva River watershed with its upland, wetland and riverine habitats provides an important wildlife corridor connecting thousands of acres of publicly owned conservation lands to the Ocala National Forest. The rivers, tributaries, associated hardwood and cypress swamps, and marshes provide food, shelter and breeding sites for many native species, including several designated as endangered, threatened, rare, or of special concern.

The wood stork, an endangered species, nests in cypress trees within the aquatic preserve, and is often observed feeding in certain shallow areas of the river. The little blue heron, tri-colored heron and limpkin, species of special concern, nest and forage along the banks of the Wekiva. Threatened plant species such as the needle palm, butterfly and water orchids, and Florida shield fern, are also found along the Wekiva. The Wekiva River has been designated an Outstanding Florida Water, a State Canoe Trail, and has been included in the federal Wild and Scenic Rivers program.

Threats

Cumulative impacts affecting water quality and quantity and loss of habitat due to existing and future over-development throughout the basin pose the greatest threat to the Wekiva River Ecosystem. The Wekiva River Protection Act (Chapter 369.301, Florida Statutes) enacted in 1988, addresses the protection of the natural resources of the Wekiva Basin. Development activities within the Protection Area must protect listed species' habitat, native vegetation, and rural character.

The habitat and other resources of the Wekiva Basin have been protected by the "rural character" of the area, characterized by open space, vast expanses of intact woodlands, low density residential areas and farmlands. Faced with tremendous growth pressures from surrounding urban areas of metropolitan Orlando, Altamonte Springs, Lake Mary and Apopka, the rural character of the Wekiva Basin is fast disappearing.

The St. Johns River

The St. Johns River is unique in that it is one of the few rivers in the world that flows north, and it is the largest river that is entirely within Florida.

The river meanders slowly from its headwaters in South Florida, approximately 300 miles to Jacksonville where it enters the Atlantic Ocean. Approximately 20 miles of the St. Johns, from Interstate 4 just west of Sanford north to State Road 44, just west of Deland are designated aquatic preserve.

The preserve consists of a diverse assemblage of plant communities such as freshwater marsh, cypress swamp, mixed hardwood swamp and hardwood hammock. The river provides food and habitat for the river otter, alligator, white ibis, great blue heron, and numerous other wading birds. The bald eagle, a threatened species, can often be observed soaring over the aquatic preserve or perched along the banks on a tree limb. A small population of the endangered West Indian manatee lives in the St. Johns River year round. Manatees are often observed during the winter months at their warm water refuge in Blue Spring Run. The importance of this winter habitat was recognized in 1978 by the Manatee Sanctuary Act, which gave legal protection to manatees at Blue Spring and other refuges throughout the state.

The sanctuary designation established restricted speed zones in portions of the St. Johns River and prohibited motor boats from Blue Spring Run

Habitats

Florida has a sandy ridge that extends down the center of the peninsula. Wekiwa Springs State Park lies just to the east of this ridge and is unique in that it has 19 distinct biological communities - more than are found in other state park in Florida.

Each of these communities supports its own distinct flora and fauna while playing host to large numbers of animals, birds and insects that can be found throughout the park. Of course, the vegetation doesn't suddenly change as you move from one habitat to another. There is a gradual transition but some habitats are much more favorable to some plants and trees than others.

The different communities are:

Mesic Flatwoods: Open canopy of widely spaced pine with a dense ground cover of herbs and shrubs. These state parks contain over 6,500 acres of mesic flatwoods occurring in a relatively continuous block in the central portion of WSSP and extend into RSRSR and the southern portion of LWRPSP.

Several variations of Mesic Flatwoods are recognized, the most common associations being:

- longleaf pine with wiregrass
- slash pine with runner oak
- gallberry with saw palmetto

Other typical plants include: St. Johns-wort, dwarf huckleberry, fetterbush, dwarf wax myrtle, stagger bush, blueberry, gopher apple, tar flower, bog buttons, blackroot, false foxglove, white-topped aster, yellow-eyed grass, and cutthroat grass.

Typical animals of Mesic Flatwoods include: oak toad, little grass frog, narrowmouth toad, black racer, red rat snake, southeastern kestrel, brown-headed nuthatch, pine warbler, Bachman's sparrow, cotton rat, cotton mouse, black bear, raccoon, gray fox, bobcat, and white-tailed deer.

Mesic Flatwoods occur on relatively flat, moderately to poorly drained terrain. The soils typically consist of 1-3 feet of acidic sands generally overlying an organic hardpan or clayey subsoil. The hardpan substantially reduces the percolation of water below and above its surface. During the rainy seasons, water frequently stands on the hardpan's surface and briefly inundates much of the flatwoods. During the drier seasons, ground water is unobtainable for many plants whose roots fail to penetrate the hardpan. Thus, many plants are under the stress of water saturation during the wet seasons and under the stress of dehydration during the dry seasons.

Fire is an important physical factor in Mesic Flatwoods. It probably occurred every 1 to 8 years during pre-Columbian times. More recently, the Mesic Flatwoods have experienced wildfires, and fire plow lines have been cut throughout the area for wildfire suppression.

The habitat conditions vary greatly primarily due to the burn histories of the areas. Nearly all plants and animals inhabiting this community are adapted to periodic fires. Several species depend on fire for their continued existence. Without relatively frequent fires, Mesic Flatwoods succeed into hardwood-dominated forests whose closed canopy can essentially eliminate the ground cover herbs and shrubs. The dense layer of litter that accumulates on unburned sites can eliminate the reproduction of pines that require a mineral soil substrate for proper germination. However, fires that are too frequent or too hot eliminate pine recruitment and may eventually transform Mesic Flatwoods into Dry Prairie.

Mesic Flatwoods are closely associated with and often grade into Wet Flat-woods, Dry Prairie, or Scrubby Flatwoods. The differences between these communities are generally related to minor topographic changes. Wet Flatwoods occupy the lower wetter areas, while Scrubby Flatwoods occupy the higher drier areas.

Mesic Flatwoods are the most widespread biological community in Florida, occupying an estimated 30 to 50 percent of the state's uplands. However, very few undisturbed areas of Mesic Flatwoods exist because of habitat mismanagement and silvicultural, agricultural, or residential development. Mesic Flatwoods are often fairly resilient, and with proper management they can generally be restored.

Sandhill: Sandy hilltops and slopes of gently rolling hills supporting longleaf pine, turkey oak, post oak, gopher apple and wiregrass. Look for sand mounds thrown up by burrowing pocket gophers.

The longleaf pine trees in the Sandhills were logged and turpentined in the 1930s and 1940s.but there were sufficient numbers left for them to regenerate throughout the sandhill. An active lightning season burn program has restored many sandhill areas, but several areas still require several restoration burns or other techniques to reach a restored status.

Sandhills are characterized as a forest of widely spaced pine trees with a sparse understory of deciduous oaks and a fairly dense ground cover of grasses and herbs on rolling hills of sand. The most typical associations are dominated by longleaf pine, turkey oak, and wiregrass. Other typical plants include bluejack oak, sand post oak, sparkleberry, persimmon, winged sumac, pinewoods dropseed, Indian grass, wild buckwheat, queen's delight, yellow foxglove, bracken fern, runner oak, goats rue, partridge pea, milk pea, dollarweeds, wild indigo, gopher apple, and golden-aster. Typical animals include tiger salamander, barking treefrog, spadefoot toad, gopher frog, gopher tortoise, worm lizard, fence lizard, mole skink, indigo snake, coachwhip snake, pine snake, short-tailed snake, crowned snake, eastern diamondback rattlesnake, bobwhite, ground dove, red-headed woodpecker, rufous-sided towhee, fox squirrel and pocket gopher.

Their soils are composed of deep, marine-deposited, yellowish sands that are well-drained and relatively sterile. The easily leached soil nutrients are brought back to the surface by the burrowing habits of some sandhill animals. Sandhills are important aquifer recharge areas because the porous sands allow water to move rapidly through with little runoff and minimal evaporation. The deep sandy soils help create a xeric environment that is accentuated by the scattered overstory, which allows more sunlight to penetrate and warm the ground. The absence of a closed canopy also allows Sandhills to cool more rapidly at night and to retain less air moisture. Thus, temperature and humidity fluctuations are generally greater in Sandhills than in nearby closed canopy forests.

Fire is a dominant factor in the ecology of this community. Sandhills are a fire maintained community, being dependent on frequent ground fires to reduce hardwood competition and to perpetuate pines and grasses. Without frequent fires, Sandhills may eventually succeed to Xeric Hammock. Unburned or cutover Sandhills may be dominated by turkey oak. The natural fire frequency appears to be every two to five years.

Sandhills are often associated with and grade into Scrub, Scrubby Flatwoods, Mesic Flatwoods, Upland Pine Forest, or Xeric Hammock. Sandhills were widespread throughout the Coastal Plain, but most have been degraded by timbering, overgrazing, plowing, fire exclusion, and other disturbances. Many have been converted to citrus groves, pastures, pine plantations, or residential and commercial developments. Thus, the importance of properly managing the remaining tracts is accentuated.

Scrub: Relatively infertile areas supporting scrub oak, saw palmetto, rusty lyonia, myrtle oak and deerberry. This the habitat favored by the endemic Florida mouse and Florida scrub-jay. The largest patch of scrub in WSSP occurs west of Sand Lake adjacent to Main Park Drive.

Scrub occurs in many forms, but is often characterized as a closed to open canopy forest of sand pines with dense clumps or vast thickets of scrub oaks and other shrubs dominating the understory. The ground cover is generally sparse, being dominated by ground lichens or, rarely, herbs. Open patches of barren sand are common. Where the overstory of sand pines is widely scattered or absent altogether, the understory and barren sands are exposed to more intense sunlight. Typical plants include sand pine, sand live oak, myrtle oak, Chapman's oak, scrub oak, saw palmetto, rosemary, rusty lyonia, ground lichens, scrub hickory, scrub palmetto, hog plum, silk bay, beak rush, milk peas, and stagger bush. Typical animals include red widow spider, scrub wolf spider, oak toad, blue-tailed mole skink, sand skink, sixlined racerunner, coachwhip, ground dove, loggerhead shrike, yellow-rumped warbler, rufous-sided towhee, and spotted skunk.

Florida scrub-jays and Florida mice are Florida endemics, which live only in scrub and scrubby flatwoods habitats.

Striped newts were discovered in 1994 in a small interior pond at Spear's Scrub. There are only 21 known sites in Florida where the striped newts exist.

Some Scrub soils are composed of well-washed, deep sands that are brilliant white at the surface; some Scrubs occur on yellow sands. The loose sands drain rapidly, creating very Xeric conditions. The plants have evolved several water conservation strategies.

Scrub is essentially a fire maintained community. Ground vegetation is extremely sparse and leaf fall is minimal, thus reducing the chance of frequent ground fires. As the sand pines mature, they retain most of their branches and build up large fuel supplies in their crowns. When a fire does occur, this fuel supply, in combination with the resinous needles and high stand density, ensures a hot, fast burning fire. Such fires allow for the regeneration of the Scrub community that might otherwise succeed to Xeric Hammock. The minerals in the vegetation are deposited on the bare sand as ashes, and the heat of the fire generally facilitates the release of pine seeds. As discerned from the life histories of the dominant plants, scrub probably burns catastrophically once every 20 to 80 years or longer.

Scrub is associated with and often grades into Sandhill, Scrubby Flatwoods, Coastal Strand, and Xeric Hammock. Scrub occurs almost exclusively in Florida, although coastal scrubs extend into adjacent Alabama and Georgia. Because Scrub occurs on high dry ground and is not an aesthetically pleasing habitat, at least to the uninitiated, this ecosystem and its many endangered and threatened species are rapidly being lost to development. Scrub is also readily damaged by off-road vehicle traffic or even foot traffic, which destroys the delicate ground cover and allows the loose sand to erode. Ground lichens may require 50 years or more to recover.

Scrubby Flatwoods: Open canopy forest of widely scattered pine trees with a sparse shrubby understory and numerous areas of barren white sand. This community is essentially a Mesic Flatwoods with a Scrub understory. Here you may also spot the Florida mouse and scrub-jay.

The vegetation is a combination of Scrub and Mesic Flatwoods species; Scrubby Flatwoods often occupy broad transitions or ecotones between these communities. Typical plants include longleaf pine, slash pine, sand live oak, Chapman's oak, myrtle oak, scrub oak, saw palmetto, staggerbush, wiregrass, dwarf blueberry, gopher apple, rusty lyonia, tarflower, golden-aster, lichens, silkbay, garberia, huckleberry, goldenrod, runner oak, pinweeds, and frostweed.

Scrubby Flatwoods generally occur intermingled with Mesic Flatwoods along slightly elevated relictual sandbars and dunes. The white sandy soil is several feet deep and drains rapidly. However, the water table is unlikely to be very deep. Scrubby Flatwoods normally do not flood even under extremely wet conditions. The temperatures and humidity of air and soil in Scrubby Flatwoods fluctuate substantially more than in most other communities because the scattered overstory, sparse understory, and barren sands of Scrubby Flatwoods do not moderate daily and seasonal changes well.

Although the elevated, deeper sandy soils of Scrubby Flatwoods engender a drier environment than the surrounding Mesic Flatwoods, the general sparsity of ground vegetation and the greater proportion of relatively incombustible scrub-oak leaf litter reduces the frequency of naturally occurring fires. Only after a long absence of fire and during periods of drought does the leaf litter become sufficiently combustible and concentrated enough to support an ecological burn. Several species of plants in Scrubby Flatwoods are typical scrub plants that endure only when long intervals between fires occur. A period of eight to 25 years between fires appears to be natural for this community. Scrubby Flatwoods are associated with and often grade into Mesic Flatwoods, Scrub, Dry Prairie or Sandhills.

Upland Mixed Forest: Well-developed, close canopy forests of upland hardwoods on rolling hills. They are most common in northern and central peninsula Florida.

Common species are the southern magnolia, pignut hickory, sweetgum, Florida maple, devil's walking stick, American hornbeam, redbud, flowering dogwood, Carolina holly, American holly, eastern hophornbeam, spruce pine, loblolly pine, live oak among others. Other typical plants include gum bumelia, hackberry, persimmon, red cedar, red mulberry, wild olive, redbay, laurel cherry, black cherry, water oak, cabbage palm, basswood, winged elm, Florida elm, sparkleberry, Hercules' club, beautyberry, partridgeberry, sarsaparilla vine, greenbrier, trilliums, beech drops, passion flower, bedstraw, strawberry bush, silverbell, caric sedges, fringe tree, horse sugar and blackgum.

Upland Mixed Forests generally lack shortleaf pine, American beech and other more northern species that typically occur in Upland Hardwood Forests most common in northern and central peninsula Florida.

Typical animals include slimy salamander, Cope's gray treefrog, bronze frog, box turtle, eastern glass lizard, green anole, broadhead skink, ground skink, red-bellied snake, gray rat snake, rough green snake, coral snake, woodcock, barred owl, pileated woodpecker, shrews, eastern mole, gray squirrel, wood rat, cotton mouse, gray fox, and white-tailed deer.

Upland Mixed Forests occur on rolling hills that often have limestone or phosphatic rock near the surface and occasionally as outcrops. Soils are generally sandy-clays or clayey sands with substantial organic and often calcareous components. The topography and clayey soils increase surface water runoff, although this is counterbalanced by the moisture retention properties of clays and by the often thick layer of leaf mulch that helps conserve soil moisture and create decidedly Mesic conditions. Furthermore, the canopy is densely closed, except during winter in areas where deciduous trees predominate. Thus, air movement and light penetration are generally low, making the humidity high and relatively constant. Because of these conditions Upland Mixed Forests rarely burn.

Upland Mixed Forests are often associated with and grade into Upland Pine Forest, Slope Forest or Xeric Hammock areas. During early stages of succession,

Upland Mixed Forests may be difficult to distinguish from Upland Pine Forests that have not been burned for several years. Disturbed sites may require hundreds of years to reach full development with species compositions representative of climax conditions. Silvicultural, agricultural, industrial, and residential developments have eliminated many of these communities. With the accelerating loss of these areas, the few remaining mature examples are in urgent need of protection and proper management.

A majority of the Upland Mixed Forests in WSSP occurs adjacent to Lake Prevatt and other wetlands and water bodies. LWRPSP contains approximately 630 acres of Upland Mixed Forest - more than any other state park in the basin. The largest areas are nested within Floodplain Forest and Hydric Hammock community types.

Xeric Hammock: Dry hardwood forests, mostly of oaks. It is characterized as either a scrubby, dense, low canopy forest with little understory other than palmetto, or a multi-storied forest of tall trees with an open or closed canopy. Several gradations between these extremes exist.

Typical plants include live oak, sand live oak, laurel oak, turkey oak, black-jack oak, red oak, sand post oak, staggerbush, saw palmetto, sparkleberry, pignut hickory, southern magnolia, redbay, American holly, wild olive, black cherry, fox grape, beautyberry, bluejack oak, Chapman's oak, persimmon, and yaupon. Typical animals include barking treefrog, spadefoot toad, gopher tortoise, worm lizard, fence lizard, black racer, red rat snake, hognose snake, crowned snake, screech-owl, turkey, blue jay, eastern mole, gray squirrel, and eastern flying squirrel.

Xeric Hammock only develops on sites that have been protected from fire for 30 or more years. It is often considered the climax community on sandy uplands. It is an advanced successional stage of Scrub or Sandhill. The variation in vegetation structure is predominantly due to the original community from which it developed. In all cases the soils consist primarily of deep, excessively-drained sands that were derived from old dune systems. Xeric Hammocks are often associated with and grade into Scrub, Sandhill, Upland Mixed Forest or Slope Forest.

The species composition of Xeric Hammock is often similar to Prairie Hammock and Maritime Hammock. The lack of herbs and the relatively incombustible oak litter make fires rare. When fire does occur, it is nearly always catastrophic and may revert a Xeric Hammock into another community type.

Xeric Hammock occurs generally as isolated patches that rarely cover large areas. Mature examples are rare, and scrub derived types have always been scarce. Being on high ground with big trees, Xeric Hammock is prime residential property, especially when near the coast. Remaining tracts of Xeric Hammock require protection from fire and development.

Baygall: Peat-filled seepage depressions with evergreen hardwoods such as sweetbay, swamp bay and loblolly bay trees with a ground canopy of sphagnum mats and ferns.

They are generally densely forested, peat-filled seepage depressions often at the base of sandy slopes. The tree canopy is composed of tall, densely packed, generally straight-boled evergreen hardwoods dominated by sweetbay, swamp red bay, and loblolly bay. A more or less open understory of shrubs and ferns commonly occurs, while sphagnum mats are often interlaced with the convoluted tree roots. Other typical plants include dahoon holly, Atlantic white cedar, fetterbush, male-berry, myrtle-leaved holly, large gallberry, wax myrtle, odorless wax myrtle, hurrah-bush, dog-hobble, white alder, possumhaw, red chokeberry, Virginia willow, laurel greenbrier, poison ivy, cinnamon fern, chain fern, wild grape, netted chain fern, sweetgum, cypress, lizard's tail, and needle palm. Typical animals include mole salamander, southern dusky salamander, southern mud salamander, opossum, southeastern shrew, short-tailed shrew, marsh rabbit, black bear, raccoon, southern mink, and bobcat.

Baygalls typically develop at the base of a slope where seepage usually maintains a saturated peat substrate. They may also be located at the edges of floodplains or in other flat areas where high lowland water tables help maintain soil moisture. The soils are generally composed of peat with an acidic pH (3.5 - 4.5).

Since Baygalls rarely dry out enough to burn, the normal fire interval in these communities is probably 50-100 years or more. After a fire, bay trees usually re-sprout from the roots and replace themselves, but severe fires may change a Baygall into a different community.

If only a small amount of surface peat is removed, a Baygall may be replaced by a Wet Flatwoods community. If the ground surface is lowered considerably, willows may invade, followed by a cypress-gum community. With recurrent fire, the site will become a shrub bog. If the subsurface peat does not burn and fire and hydrological regimes are undisturbed, a burned out bay forest may be replaced by a stand of white cedar.

Baygall is often associated with and may grade into Seepage Slope, Floodplain Forest or Floodplain Swamp. The species composition of Baygalls frequently overlaps with Bog, Dome Swamp, Basin Swamp, Strand Swamp, Bottomland Forest, Wet Flatwoods, and Hydric Hammock.

Since Baygalls need seepage flows and a high water tables, alterations in the local hydrology may impact Baygall communities. They may also need fire protection during droughts, especially if water tables are lowered. Baygalls are vulnerable to logging, peat mining, and conversion to agricultural land. When drained, the peat soils are valued for farming, although they then begin to oxidize and disappear. The renewed interest in mining peat as fuel may place greater pressure on these wetlands.

Depression Marshes: Usually the result of sinkholes, they support their own micro-habitats. Plants like wax myrtle and buttonbush thrive here.

Depression Marsh is characterized as a shallow, usually rounded depression in sand substrate with herbaceous vegetation often in concentric bands. Typical plants include St. John's wort, spikerush, yelloweyed grass, chain fern, willows, maidencane, wax myrtle, swamp primrose, bloodroot, buttonbush, fire flag, pickerelweed, arrowheads, and bladderwort. Larger and more permanent Depression Marshes may have many of the same plants and animals listed as typical of Basin Marshes.

Depression Marshes are important breeding and foraging areas for species such as the flatwoods salamander, mole salamander, tiger salamander, dwarf salamander, striped newt, oak toad, cricket frog, pinewoods treefrog, barking treefrog, squirrel treefrog, little grass frog, southern chorus frog, ornate chorus frog, narrowmouth toad, eastern spadefoot toad, gopher frog, white ibis, wood stork and sandhill crane. Depression Marshes occurring as isolated wetlands within larger upland ecosystems are critical for many additional wetland and upland animals. Because of isolation and small size, many Depression Marshes support very different species than those found in larger, more permanent wetlands that may have many of the plants and animals typical to Basin Marshes.

Depression Marshes are typical of karst regions where sand has slumped around or over a sinkhole creating a conical depression that then filled by direct rain fall, runoff, or seepage from uplands. The substrate is usually acid sand with deepening peat toward the center. Some depressions may have developed or be maintained by a subsurface hardpan. Hydrological conditions vary, with most Depression Marshes drying in most years.

Hydroperiods range widely from as few as 50 days or less to more than 200 days per year.

Fire is important to maintaining this community type by restricting invasion of shrubs and trees and the formation of peat. Fire frequency is often greatest around the periphery of the marsh and least toward the center. A severe peat fire can lower the ground surface and create a pond at the marsh center.

Depression Marshes are often associated with and grade into Wet Prairie, Seepage Slope, Wet Flatwoods, Mesic Flatwoods, Dome Swamp or Bog. They may also occur in association with various types of lakes, such as Sandhill Lake or Flatwoods Lake.

Depression Marshes are threatened by drainage, agriculture, pollution, fire suppression, and invasion of exotic species. Depression Marshes may be filled and converted to other uses. Lowering water tables may eliminate many. Some on public lands have been deepened by explosives to allow for stocking with game fish. By preying upon the eggs and larvae of frogs and salamanders, these fish may eliminate the amphibians that depend on such seasonal wetlands for successful reproduction. Likewise, many species of invertebrates not adapted to predation by fishes may be eliminated.

Dome Swamp: Shallow, forested, usually circular depressions, generally presenting a domed profile because smaller trees grow in the shallower waters at the outer edge, while bigger trees grow in the deeper water in the interior. Pond cypress, swamp tupelo, and slash pine are common plants.

Other typical plants include red maple, dahoon holly, swamp bay, sweetbay, loblolly bay, pond apple, Virginia willow, fetterbush, chain fern, netted chain fern, poison ivy, laurel greenbrier, Spanish moss, wild pine, royal fern, cinnamon fern, coastal plain willow, maidencane, orchids, wax myrtle, swamp titi, St. John's wort, sawgrass, lizard's tail, swamp primrose, water hyssop, redroot, sphagnum moss, floating heart, buttonbush, arum, and fire flag.

Typical animals include flatwoods salamander, mole salamander, dwarf salamander, oak toad, southern cricket frog, pinewoods treefrog, little grass frog, narrowmouth toad, alligator, snapping turtle, striped mud turtle, mud turtle, eastern mud snake, cottonmouth, woodstork, wood duck, swallow-tailed kite, barred owl, pileated woodpecker, great-crested flycatcher, prothonotory warbler, and rusty blackbird.

Dome Swamps typically develop in sandy flatwoods and in karst areas where sand has slumped around or over sinkholes, creating conical depressions. Soils are composed of peat, which becomes thickest toward the center of the domes, and are generally underlain with acidic sands and then limestone, although other subsoils may occur.

Dome Swamps often receive much water from runoff, but many are connected with underground channels that are the main water sources. Water is typically present for 200 to 300 days per year, being deepest and longest lasting near the centers. Some Dome Swamps have clay (bowl shaped bottoms) lens that help retain water. During drought periods Dome Swamps help recharge the aquifer as water tables drop.

Somewhat deeper than normal water levels are not likely to do much harm, but extended wet periods limit tree growth and prevent reproduction. Shortened wet periods permit invasion of mesophytic species, which change the character of the understory and eventually allow hardwoods to replace cypress.

Dome Swamps typically grade into Wet Prairie or Marl Prairie around the periphery, but may be bordered by Bottomland Forest or Swale. Species frequently overlaps with those of Strand Swamp, Wet Flatwoods, Basin Swamp, Baygall, Floodplain Swamp, and Freshwater Tidal Swamp

Fire is essential for the maintenance of a cypress dome community. Fires most frequency occur at the dryer outer edges of the domes since the interiors are deep peat and moist most of the year. The normal fire cycle may be as short as three to five years along the outer edges and as long as 100 to 150 years towards the centers. The profile of a Dome Swamp (i.e., smaller trees at the periphery and largest trees near the center) is largely due to fire killing plants and trees around the outer edges.

Without periodic fires, hardwood invasion and peat accumulation, convert the dome to Bottomland Forest or Bog. Dome Swamps dominated by bays are close to this transition.

Cypress is very tolerant of light surface fires, but muck fires burning into the peat can kill them, lower the ground surface, and transform a dome into a pond. Dome Swamps may also be degraded by pollution and the invasion of exotic plants.

A dome swamp exists in the Lower Wekiva River State Preserve along its western border with Seminole State Forest.

Floodplain Marsh: Wetlands of herbaceous vegetation and low shrubs that occur in river floodplains on sandy alluvial soils with considerable peat accumulation.

They are found along the St. Johns River in the Lower Wekiva River State Preserve and other Central Florida areas. They also occur along the Kissimmee and Myakka rivers.

Emergent grasses, herbs, and shrubs that dominate Floodplain Marshes include sawgrass, maidencane, and buttonbush. Other typical plants include sand cordgrass, dotted smartweed, arrowheads, pickerelweed, reimargrass, spikerush, bulrushes, bladderpod, common reed, coreopsis, glasswort, seashore dropseed, sea purslane, and water primrose.

Typical animals include cricket frog, pig frog, leopard frog, American alligator, eastern mud snake, banded water snake, striped swamp snake, great blue heron, great egret, snowy egret, little blue heron, tricolored heron, black-crowned night-heron, yellow-crowned night-heron, northern harrier, sandhill crane, raccoon, and river otter.

Floodplain Marshes are maintained by water and fire. They have flowing water for about 250 days per year. Shorter wet periods permit invasion by shrubs resulting in marsh loss. Fires seem to occur naturally every one to five-year maintaining an open herbaceous community by restricting shrub invasion, however, during drought periods severe fires often burn the mucky peat.

Floodplain Marshes are associated with, and often grade into, Wet Prairie or Riverine communities. They eventually succeed to Bog, if succession is not reversed by muck fires.

Many marsh areas have been degraded by pollution or destroyed by drainage for agriculture.

Floodplain Swamp: Wet forests and woodlands that border a river and are often flooded. They occur on flooded soils along stream channels and in low spots and oxbows within river floodplains. They are extremely prevalent along the west shore of the Wekiva River and the St. Johns River.

Many plants and animals, onsite and down river, depend on the natural fluctuations of the swamps for survival and reproduction. The species composition is frequently similar to that of the Slough, Strand Swamp, Dome Swamp, and Basin Swamp communities.

Dominant trees are usually buttressed hydrophytic trees such as cypress and tupelo. The understory and ground cover are generally sparse. Other typical plants include ogeechee tupelo, water tupelo, swamp titi, wax myrtle, dahoon holly, myrtle-leaved holly, large gallberry, possumhaw, hurrah-bush, white alder, lizard's tail, leather fern, royal fern, marsh fern, soft rush, laurel greenbrier, hazel alder, hawthorn, and swamp privet.

A diversity of temporary and permanent residents animals is supported. They include marbled salamander, mole salamander, amphiuma, Alabama waterdog, Southern dusky salamander, two-lined salamander, three-lined salamander, dwarf salamander, slimy salamander, rusty mud salamander, southern toad, cricket frog, birdvoiced treefrog, gray treefrog, bullfrog, river frog, Southern leopard frog, alligator, river cooter, stinkpot, Southeastern five-lined skink, broadhead skink, mud snake, rainbow snake, redbelly water snake, brown water snake, glossy crayfish snake, black swamp snake, cottonmouth, yellow-crowned night-heron, wood duck, swallowtail kite, Mississippi kite, red-shouldered hawk, woodcock, barred owl, chimney swift, hairy woodpecker, pileated woodpecker, Acadian flycatcher, Carolina wren, veery, white-eyed vireo, red-eyed vireo, parula warbler, prothonotary warbler, hooded warbler, Swainson's warbler, cardinal, towhee, opossum, southeastern shrew, short-tailed shrew, beaver, wood rat, rice rat, cotton mouse, golden mouse, bear, raccoon, and bobcat.

Flooding occurs for most of the year, with sites along channels covered by aerobic flowing water while sloughs and backswamps are flooded with anerobic water. Seasonal and often prolonged flooding restricts the growth of most shrubs and herbs, leaving most of the ground surface open or thinly mantled with leaf litter. These swamps are usually too wet to support fire.

Soils of Floodplain Swamps are highly variable mixtures of sand, organic, and alluvial materials, although some sites, especially within sloughs, or on smaller streams, may have considerable peat accumulation. Floods redistribute detrital accumulations to other portions of the floodplain or into the main river channel. This rich organic debris is essential to the functional integrity of downriver ecosystems such as estuaries.

Floodplain Swamps are often associated with and grade into Floodplain Forest or Hydric Hammock, and occasionally Baygall. Alteration of the wet period by impoundments or river diversions and the disruption of floodplain communities by forestry or agriculture have devastating consequences to entire river and bay systems.

Hydric Hammock: Lowlands, usually wet but rarely flooded. They are inland from river swamps or associated with springs or karst seepages. They have thick forests of deciduous hardwoods and cabbage and needle palms, laurel and water oak, red mulberry and sweetbay, with variable understory often dominated by palms and ferns. They are often difficult to differentiate from Bottomland Forest, Prairie Hammock, and Floodplain Forest.

Other typical plants are diamond-leaf oak, red cedar, red maple, swamp bay, southern magnolia, wax myrtle, saw palmetto, bluestem palmetto, needle palm, poison ivy, dahoon holly, myrsine, hackberry, sweetgum, loblolly pine, Florida elm, swamp chestnut oak, American hornbeam, Walter viburnum, royal fern, peppervine, rattanvine, yellow jessamine, and Virginia creeper. Typical animals are green anole, flycatchers, warblers, and gray squirrel. They are good areas to see barred owls and pileated woodpeckers.

Hydric Hammocks occur where limestone may be near the surface and frequently outcrops. Soils are sands with considerable organic material that, although generally saturated, are flooded for short periods following heavy rains and seldom flood more than 60 days per year. Because of the generally saturated soil and the sparse herbaceous ground cover, they rarely burn.

If a Hydric Hammock water table drops, it will gradually change to mesic conditions. If the hammock is flooded, many trees will die and eventually be replaced by more hydrophytic species. Hydric Hammocks generally grade into Floodplain Swamp, Strand Swamp, Basin Swamp, Baygall, Wet Flatwoods, Coastal Berm, Maritime Hammock, Slope Forest, Upland Mixed Forest, or Upland Hardwood Forest.

WSSP has over 2,800 acres of Hydric Hammock. Southern pine beetles affected much of this area from May to September of 2001 due to the predominance of old loblolly pine trees. Approximately 300 cypress trees were planted along Mill Creek in 2002.

RSRSR has over 5,780 acres of Hydric Hammock. Hand ferns, a rare species, are known to occur epiphytically on cabbage palms in the southern portions of Reserve. There are over 3,600 acres of Hydric Hammock in LWRPSP.

Wet Flatwoods: A hardpan layer of soil supporting a variety of plants able to withstand flooding when a river overflows and severe summer droughts. The flat, poorly drained soils typically consist of 1 to 3 feet of acidic sands generally overlying organic hardpan or clay restricting the percolation of water below and above its surface.

They have open-canopy forests of scattered pine trees or cabbage palms with either thick shrubby understory and very sparse ground cover, or a sparse understory and a dense ground cover of hydrophytic herbs and shrubs. Variations exist between these extremes. Cabbage palm flatwoods tend to occur on more circumneutral sands (pH 6.0 - 7.5) underlain by marl or shell beds.

Common plants are pine forests, palmetto, shiny lyonia, gallberry and pond, slash, loblolly and longleaf pine. Other typical plants are sweetbay, spikerush, beakrush, sedges, dwarf wax myrtle, gallberry, titi, creeping beggarweed, deer tongue, gay feather, greenbrier, bluestem, and pitcher plants.

Typical animals include oak toad, cricket frog, chorus frog, black racer, yellow rat snake, diamondback rattlesnake, pygmy rattlesnake, red-shouldered hawk, bobwhite, opossum, cottontail rabbit, cotton rat, cotton mouse, raccoon, striped skunk, bobcat, and white-tailed deer.

Pine densities vary greatly throughout the river basin. Areas near Rock Springs Run have dense small diameter pines, while areas towards the center of RSRSR have more widely spaced, larger diameter pines. Many vegetative differences are probably due to differences in burning and logging.

In rainy seasons, water often inundates flatwoods for a month or more each year. During the drier seasons, water is less accessible for plants whose roots fail to penetrate the hardpan. Thus, many plants have periods of water saturation stress and dehydration stress.

During pre-Columbian times fires probably occurred every three to 10 years. Nearly all plants and animals inhabiting this community are adapted to periodic fires, and several species depend on fires for their continued existence. Without fire there is an accumulation of needle drape and the height of the flammable understory shrubs increases, thus increasing the probability of a catastrophic canopy fire. Without relatively frequent fires, Wet Flatwoods succeed into Hardwood Forests whose closed canopies eliminate ground cover herbs and shrubs.

Wet Flatwoods are closely associated with and often grade into Hydric Hammock, Mesic Flatwoods, Wet Prairie, or Basin Swamp. Wet Flatwoods may also grade into Dome Swamp or Strand Swamp, but the absence of a Wet Prairie ecotone suggests that the hydrology has been disturbed.

Wet Flatwoods, once common in Coastal Plains, are now rare with intact overstory and understory, without exotics, and with the potential for maintenance by fire. They recover well from overstory damage but recover poorly when the ground cover or hydrology changes. Exotic plants readily invade Wet Flatwoods in south Florida. Controlling exotics takes prompt action.

Marsh Lake: Naturally occurring shallow lakes - such as Lake Prevatt - whose water levels fluctuate wildly and may even dry up at times.

Typical plants include spikerush, yelloweyed grasses, St. John's wort, chain fern, coastal plain willow, maidencane, wax myrtle, water primrose, floating heart, buttonbush, fire flag, pickerelweed, arrowhead, bladderworts, bottlebrush threeawn, toothache grass, star rush, bulrushes, sawgrass, and nut sedge.

Many animals utilize marshes primarily for feeding and breeding areas but spend most of their time in other habitats. Animals more dependent on marshes, spend most of their time within them. Typical animals include amphiuma, lesser siren, greater siren, cricket frog, green treefrog, bullfrog, pig frog, leopard frog, alligator, eastern mud snake, banded water snake, green water snake, striped crayfish snake, black swamp snake, American bittern, least bittern, great blue heron, great egret, snowy egret, little blue heron, tricolored heron, green-backed heron, black-crowned night-heron, white ibis, glossy ibis, bald eagle, northern harrier, king rail, Virginia rail, sora, limpkin, long-billed marsh wren, yellowthroat, red-winged blackbird, boat tailed grackle, and Florida water rat.

The depressions in which these communities develop were typically formed by (1) surface sands slumping into solution holes formed in the underlying limestone causing circular depressions; or (2) during higher sea levels, currents, waves, and winds scoured depressions that were left after the seas regressed. Soils in these depressions generally consist of acidic sands with some peat and occasionally a clay bowl.

Water comes mostly from immediately surrounding uplands runoff. The lakes help recharge the aquifer when water tables drop during drought periods. Water generally remains throughout the year in a Marsh Lake, although water levels may fluctuate substantially.

Sandhill Upland Lake: Generally small permanent water bodies in shallow rounded depressions occurring in sandy upland communities. They allow amphibians (including the striped newt and Florida gopher frog) with fish-free areas to reproduce.

They are typically still water bodies without significant surface inflows or outflows. Water may be largely come from lateral ground water seepage from well-drained uplands and/or from artesian sources via the underlying limestone aquifer. Water levels may fluctuate substantially, sometimes becoming completely dry during droughts.

Vegetation may be largely restricted to a narrow band along the shore, composed of aquatic grasses and herbs or a dense shrub thicket, depending on fire frequency and water fluctuations. Shallow, gradually sloping shorelines may have much broader bands of emergent vegetation with submerged aquatic plants dominating much of the water. Floating plants may cover much of the surface.

Typical plants include panicums, rushes, bladderwort, water lilies, sawgrass, pickerelweed, fragrant waterlily, water shield, St. John's wort, arrowheads, beak rush, yellow-eyed grass, hatpins, meadow-beauty, sundews, and spikerush.

The lakes are important breeding areas for terrestrial amphibians, including the striped newt and threatened gopher frog, as well as many unusual or endemic insects. They are important watering holes for many mammals and birds inhabiting the surrounding xeric communities. Wading birds and ducks may use the lakes as feeding areas.

The soil is primarily sand with organic deposits increasing with water depth. The water tends to be clear, neutral to slightly acidic, moderately soft with varying mineral content. The water may be high in oxygen, with extremely low nutrient levels, seldom becoming eutrophic unless artificially fertilized by human-related activities.

Sandhill Upland Lakes are extremely affected by ground water levels. Municipal, industrial and agricultural withdrawals of ground water may lower regional water tables, causing successional responses. Groundwater pollution, especially from misapplications of chemicals on surrounding well-drained uplands, may alter the nutrient balance and produce devastating effects on the fauna and flora. Because they frequently have direct or indirect connections with the aquifer, Sandhill Upland Lakes often function as aquifer recharge areas and, thus, should be protected from pollution. Invasion by exotic species is also an important concern in Sandhill Upland Lake communities.

Blackwater Stream: Streams receiving surface water runoff from sandy wetlands where organic soils act as reservoirs, collecting rainfall and discharging it slowly.

The Wekiva and Rock Springs Runs mix with tea-colored surface runoff, resulting in blackwater. The entire lower reach of the Wekiva River (below Rock Springs Run) is mapped as blackwater stream and all portions of the St. Johns River, within the park boundaries, are similarly labeled. Also, the lower reaches of Blackwater Creek flow through the Lower Wekiva River Preserve State Park.

The tea-colored waters of Blackwater Streams are laden with tannins, particulates, and dissolved organic matter and iron derived from drainage through swamps and marshes. They generally are acidic (pH = 4.0 - 6.0), but may become neutral or slightly alkaline during low rain periods since the groundwater is alkaline. Water temperatures may fluctuate substantially, generally with the air temperature.

The dark water reduces light penetration, inhibiting photosynthesis and the growth of submerged plants. Emergent and floating aquatic vegetation may occur along shallower and slower moving sections, but is often sparse because of steep banks and considerable seasonal fluctuations in water levels.

Typical plants include golden club, smartweed, sedges, and grasses. Typical animals include river longnose gar, gizzard shad, threadfin shad, redfin pickerel, chain pickerel, ironcolor shiner, Ohoopee shiner, weed shiner, blacktail shiner, chubsucker, channel catfish, banded topminnow, pygmy killifish mosquitofish, mud sunfish, flier, everglades pygmy sunfish, banded sunfish, redbreast sunfish, dollar sunfish, stumpknocker, spotted bass, black crappie, darters, Alabama waterdog, river frog, alligator, snapping turtle, alligator snapping turtle, river cooter, Florida cooter, peninsula cooter, stinkpot, spiny softshell, red-belly watersnake, brown watersnake, beaver, and river otter.

Blackwater Streams have sandy bottoms overlain by organics and frequently underlain by limestone. Limestone outcrops may also occur. Blackwater Streams generally lack the continuous extensive floodplains and natural levees of Alluvial Streams. Instead, they typically have high, steep banks alternating with Floodplain Swamps. High banks confine water movement except during major floods. The absence of significant quantities of suspended sediments reduces their ability to construct natural levees.

Many of the rivers in the southeast Coastal Plain are Blackwater Streams. Very few, however, have escaped major disturbances and alteration. Clear-cutting adjacent forested lands is one of the more devastating alterations for this community. Additionally, the limited buffering capacity of Blackwater Streams intensifies the detrimental impacts of agricultural and industrial effluents.

Spring-run Streams: Fed by groundwater and vulnerable to infestation by exotic plants.

Spring-run Streams are perennial and derive most, if not all, their water from artesian openings in the underground aquifer. Aquifer water is generally clear, neutral to slightly alkaline (pH = 7.0 - 8.2), perennially cool (66 - 75°F) and saturated with important minerals. These conditions allow light to penetrate deeply and limit the effects of environmental fluctuations thus, helping plants to grow.

Spring-run Streams are among the most productive aquatic habitats. Typical plants include tape grass, wild rice, giant cutgrass, arrowheads, southern naiads, pondweeds, and chara. Typical animals include mollusks, stoneflies, mayflies, caddisflies, simuliids, chironomids, American alligator, alligator snapping turtle, Suwannee cooter, loggerhead musk turtle, rainbow snake, red-belly watersnake, brown watersnake, and many fishes.

Spring-run Streams generally have sand bottoms or exposed limestone along their central channel. Calcareous silts may form thick deposits in quiet shallow zones, while leaf drift and other debris collect around fallen trees and quiet basins. If undisturbed, submerged aquatic vegetation may cover stream bottoms and provides shelter and abundant food for aquatic life. The quiet, areas along with limestone outcrops and rock debris, form important aquatic habitats for small aquatic organisms.

The water emanating from the aquifer is generally clear because of the filtering and absorbing actions of the soils and aquifer limestone through which the water percolates and flows. Deep water may appear bluish due to light-refraction, similar to the sky appearing blue. If the water sources for the aquifer are substantially influenced by nearby swamps or flatwoods, the spring-run may temporarily become stained with tannins and other dissolved organics during or following periods of heavy rains.

When extensive underground cavities connect the spring caverns with nearby sinks and swallow holes, the spring-run may become turbid with suspended particulates during, and following, heavy rains and floods. Conversely, during periods of low rainfall, the aquifer can become supersaturated with calcium, carbonates, and other ions. These chemicals readily precipitate when the water reaches the surface, causing the spring-head or boil to appear milky.

Human-related impacts include:

- Withdrawal of substantial amounts of aquifer water within a spring flow recharge area may reduce or eliminate the spring flow. Normal flow rates may return when excessive withdrawals are eliminated.

- Applying agricultural, residential, and industrial pollutants that may leach through soils, especially when improperly applied or disposed. If polluted groundwater infiltrates the deep aquifer feeding Spring-run Streams, recovery may not be possible.

- Applying herbicides for controlling aquatic plants that may cause eutrophication of streams.

Destruction of aquatic vegetation by over use or misuse. Overuse will increase because of the increasing number of people enjoying the clean, cool, spring water. A delicate balance between recreation and preservation must be sought.

Introduction of exotic plants and animals are often severely detrimental to native species, and may disrupt recreational activities. Exotic plants, mostly wild taro, are a major problem along Rock Springs Run and the Wekiva River.

Aquatic Cave: Aquatic and Terrestrial Caves are cavities below the ground surface in karst areas. A cave system may contain both Aquatic (water filled) and Terrestrial areas. The limestone aquifers that underlie the entire state of Florida are largely vast Aquatic Cave communities.

There are two cave entrances in Wekiwa Springs. About 600 feet of passage was explored via the smaller vent in 1999. The main vent has had little exploration due to the extreme water flow. The main entrance, a vertical fissure and a horizontal vent, is located on the southeastern corner of the basin. The smaller vent resembles a horizontal bedding plane. The caves are home to the Orlando cave crayfish and several unknown species of cave isopods.

Aquatic Caves are generally stable environments having constant temperatures and clear deep bluish water. The water may become brown from tannins, leached from decaying plants, carried in with rainwater. The water may become milky white if fine limestone mud from the bottom of the cave is suspended in the water column following a disturbance. A bottom substrate of organic silts can also muddy the water with suspended particles.

Waters are generally neutral to alkaline with a high mineral content (particularly calcium bicarbonate and magnesium). However, flowing water within Aquatic Caves generally has a lower pH, is often under-saturated with carbonates, and has a relatively richer fauna. Cave water characteristics may vary seasonally due to inputs from surface streams, or because of detrital pulses and other surface inputs during periods of substantial aquifer recharge.

The areas around cave entrances may be densely vegetated. Within the cave, illumination levels and thus, vegetation densities drop rapidly with increased distance from the entrance. Within the limits of light penetration, called the twilight zone, species of algae, mosses, liverworts, and an occasional fern or herbaceous plant may grow. Beyond the twilight zone, plants are generally absent or limited to a few inconspicuous species of fungi that grow on guano or other organic debris

Animals inhabiting Subterranean Natural Communities are generally divided into three groups according to their cave adaptations: trogloxenes, troglophiles, and troglobites. Trogloxenes spend much of their lives in caves, but must periodically go to the surface to feed or breed. Woodrats, harvestmen, cave crickets, some salamanders, and many species of bats are typical examples.

Troglophiles generally live in caves, but may also live in surface areas with moist microhabitats. Cave orb spiders, and some crickets, fish and salamanders are typical examples.

Troglobites (also called phreatobites) evolved to survive in deep, totally dark Aquatic caves. They are dependent on detrital inputs and other nutrients imported from the surface, thus, well-developed life forms generally are limited to karst areas with surface connections.

Typical troglobites include blind cave crayfish, blind cave salamander, cave amphipods, cave shrimp, cave snail, and cave isopods. Troglobites found in some north Florida Terrestrial Caves are cave mites, some cave spiders, springtail and a cave earwig.

Though they never leave their cave environments, troglobites and troglophiles depend on outside energy sources, such as detritus that washes in through sinkholes and other cave entrances. Fecal materials from trogloxenes that feed outside caves are also important nutrients for troglobites.

The two main geologic processes forming caves are: phreatic and vadose. Phreatic processes occur below the aquifer's surface where ground water is confined and subjected to hydrostatic pressure. Vadose processes occur at the top of or above the aquifer, where air enters the passageways and water flows freely under the influence of gravity. In both processes, the dissolution and corrosion of limestone play roles in enlarging cave passageways.

These forces differ primarily in the slopes of the passageways that result. Phreatic passageways are generally circular or elliptic, while vadose passageways are more triangular with a broad base of the triangle at the bottom. All limestone caves begin under phreatic conditions. As water tables drop, vadose conditions replace phreatic conditions. If water later rises, the processes reverse. During Pleistocene and other geologic times, Florida water tables fluctuated substantially with sea levels, resulting in caves developing both phreatic and vadose characteristics, thus, Terrestrial and Aquatic Caves often occur together.

Terrestrial Caves may occur at the bottoms of dry sinkholes, ancient (dry) springs swallow holes or what were Aquatic Caves, exposed due to low water tables. Typically they exhibit aquatic conditions during periods of heavy rainfall. Terrestrial Caves may harbor relatively permanent pools or lakes that formed in natural depressions from buildup of rimstone, or where the aquifer inundates the lower cavities.

Terrestrial Caves are stable environments, having relatively constant temperatures and humidity. Within a cave, conditions vary with locations; a twilight zone (nearest to the light source) is generally warmer and experiences more temperature and humidity fluctuations than does a middle zone or dark zone that circulates air due to "cave breathing." A deep zone is the most stable zone because the air is essentially static.

Terrestrial Cave faunas vary according to the zones, with trogloxenes being more common in the twilight and middle zones, and troglobites being more common in the deep zone. Pools fed by seepage or dripping water generally have a higher pH, are high in dissolved carbonates, low in organic matter suitable for food, and have sparse fauna.

Terrestrial Cave subterranean Natural Communities are extremely fragile. Their faunas are adapted to very stable environments and have a limited ability to survive minor environmental changes. Cave entrance alterations may affect detrital input levels and cause changes in air circulation patterns and the cave microclimate. Spelunkers entering into a bat roosting, maternity, or hibernation caves may cause abandonment by bats, losing an important energy source for the cave ecosystem.

Aquatic Caves are threatened by pollution of ground and surface waters from agricultural, industrial, and residential sources, as well as by disturbances from divers. The unique troglobitic species generally have very low population levels and can be severely impacted by over-collection and by pollution in incoming surface water. Environmental management procedures are needed to protect these fragile communities.

Sinkhole (synonyms: lime sink, sink, solution pit, cenote, grotto, doline, chimney hole, banana hole).

Sinkholes are generally cylindrical or conical depressions with steep limestone walls. Those which drain quickly and only contain water following heavy rains are

called Sinkholes, while those which contain water most of the year and dry only during extreme droughts are called Sinkhole Lakes. The differences are often subtle and an area may have both if the upper portions of the limestone are typically above water, and the lower portions are typically below water.

Sinkhole vegetation may be that of a well developed forest where sands cover the rock and/or moderately sloped sides. Such conditions are typically confined to the upper portions and around the rim. With steeper rock walls, soils accumulate in cracks and crevices, generally becoming covered by mosses, liverworts, and ferns with occasional herbs and shrubs in crevices. Sinkholes provide habitat for relictual populations of many species of salamanders and invertebrates that would not survive in drier areas.

Typical plants include southern magnolia, sweetgum, wax myrtle, wild grape, Virginia creeper, poison ivy, partridgeberry, greenbrier, water oak, flowering dogwood, horse sugar, sparkleberry, diamond-leaf oak, live oak, hophornbeam, tupelo, white ash, Florida maple, pignut hickory, beautyberry, and gum bumelia. Steep rock walls are more or less covered by a variety of mosses, liverworts, ferns and sometimes herbs, including such rare and threatened species as Venus'-hair fern and halberd fern.

Sinkholes are most common in karst areas where the underlying limestone has been riddled with solution cavities by the chemical and physical actions of underground waters. The cavities become interconnected, large underwater caverns. When water tables drop, cavern roofs lose water pressure support and portions may collapse, leaving deep cylindrical or conical surface depressions. Organic and mineral debris collapsing into a cavity may partially block (generally not completely) the hole to the water. Some Sinkholes are the relics of ancient springs or swallowholes that have become dry due to lowered ground water.

Sinkholes generally have very moist microclimates. The depressions help protect Sinkholes from drying winds, and surrounding trees often form nearly complete canopies providing shelter from intensive insolation. Seepage from surrounding uplands may slowly moisten the walls and the frequent presence of standing water contributes high humidity. These conditions may also buffer temperature, allowing a unique mixture of tropical and temperate flora to exist in many Florida Sinkholes.

Sinkholes and Sinkhole Lakes often help support other Lacustrine and Palustrine communities, including Dome Swamp; Depression Marsh; and Sandhill Upland, Flatwoods and Prairie Lakes. When several Sinkholes coalesce, Basin Marsh or Swamp and Clastic Upland, Marsh or Swamp Lakes may eventually develop. Thus, the distinctions between Sinkhole communities and other related communities are frequently subtle, as one very gradually succeeds to another.

The fragile microclimate communities of Sinkholes are easily damaged by:

- Large withdrawals of groundwater that lower water levels, reducing the hydroperiods of Sinkhole Lakes.

- Swimming in Sinkhole Lakes, disturbing the aquatic community.

- Soil disturbances in close uplands that affect water seepage.

- Foot traffic and dirt bikes that subject flora to trampling and erosion of steep walls.

- Over-collection of lush, unique flora.

- Use as a dumpsites.

- Logging which increases both insolation and sedimentation levels.

- Invasion of exotic plants that replace native plants.

Since sinkholes are conduits to the aquifer and frequently aid in aquifer recharge, ground water quality is easily affected by chemical applications, waste treatments, and spills on the surrounding upland. Close monitoring is needed to determine potential pollution impacts and mitigation needs.

Ruderal: These are areas where past or present human uses (logging, farming etc.) have impacted the natural state of the land.

Fire

Fire is not only a natural process it is also an essential one for many Florida habitats such as Sandhills, Pine Flatwoods, Scrub and Marsh. For thousands of years fires have been ignited by lightning strikes.

Fire is essential for plant regeneration in many areas of the park. That is why carefully-planned and executed prescribed burns are carried out today. Without fire these communities change and the plants and animals unique to them are lost. Without fire, oaks and other vegetation can quickly overtake these communities. Fires also help kill insects and prevent disease from spreading through a forest.

Today, prescribed burns are carried out by staff and these are still an essential ingredient in maintaining the health of Scrubland, Sandhills and Pine Flatwoods. Prescribed burns also reduce the chance of wildfires.

More than 4,000 years ago Native Americans used fire to help hunting. Fires drove animals to areas where they could be more easily killed. Prescribed burns take place almost year-round depending on conditions. Many plants have adapted to natural burns and within days of a fire, you will spot new green shoots sprouting everywhere. Fox squirrels, gopher tortoises, scrub jays, red-cockaded woodpeckers, wiregrass and longleaf pines are just a few of the many species which depend on fire.

Longleaf pines have a thick bark which protects them from the flames. Longleaf pine is so fire resistant that the trees are hardly damaged by the fire. Its seedlings remain in a "grass stage" for several years. A bristle of green needles is all that can be seen above ground but below the seedling is pushing its taproot dozens of feet below ground. Once the fire has passed the seedling starts a furious growth spurt fuelled by its long tap root. The sapling can grow three to four feet in the first year, enough to raise the bud above the next low level fire.

Sandpine cones remain closed until the intense heat of a fire opens them and allows the seeds to fall out. The seeds are then able to start life in an area cleared of other vegetation and with added nutrients provided by the ash from the burned vegetation.

Smaller plants use the soil as an insulating layer and produce new growth from underground roots. Wiregrass is one of these plants and is usually the first to send up new shoots after a fire.

Most large animals can outrun a fire while smaller ones such as mice, snakes, lizards and turtles, usually take shelter underground in burrows.

Florida is often referred to as the lightning capital of the world and many wild fires are caused by lightning strikes.

These strikes often hit the ground outside the area of rainfall or ignite dry fuel that smolders through the rain shower and then begins to burn once the rain has stopped.

More than 100,000 wildfires are reported in the United States every year with about 7,000 occurring in Florida although lightning only accounts for about 20 percent of these fires. Careless campers and thoughtless smokers throwing lit cigarettes away cause other fires or they are started deliberately.

Exploring The Parks

Wekiwa Springs State Park

Sand Lake is a borrow pit constructed in the mid-1960s. The pit was flooded when an artesian spring was uncovered. Inflow to the lake is primarily through the artesian spring and surface runoff. Sand Lake drains into the Wekiwa lagoon through an unnamed creek just below the bridge across the main springs.

Lake Prevatt is perhaps the largest hydrologic feature of Wekiwa Springs State Park. This natural lake is located on the southwestern edge of WSSP A small outcove of the lake lies outside the park boundary. Current information suggests it is not spring-fed. Its water level is closely tied to precipitation and runoff from urban areas located to the west and south of the park.

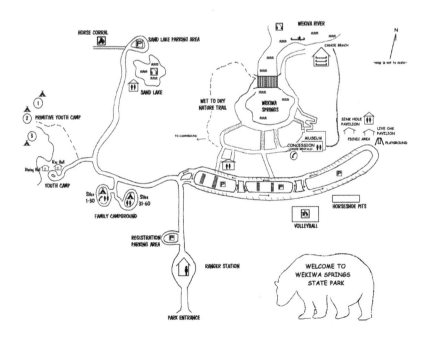

Due to development, surface water enters the park in larger quantities, and much more quickly following storms, then it once did. The effect of precipitation and runoff on the lake was shown in 2002; due to an extended drought early in the year, the lake contained virtually no surface water, yet in September, surface levels approached the maximum. The effect runoff from developed areas has on this system is unknown.

Anthropogenic hydrologic alterations such as have occurred in the Lake Prevatt area are expected to have significant impact on many Wekiva Basin ecosystems.

Recreation Facilities • Swimming • Restrooms • Picnic Area
Children's Play Area • Volley Ball • Trails • Hiking/ Nature (13mi)
Equestrian (8mi) • Biking (9mi) • Multi-use (37mi) • Canoe (8mi)

Markham Woods
Benches • Interpretive Kiosks

Rock Springs Run State Reserve

The park is bordered on the south by Rock Springs Run and to the east the Wekiva River is within the boundary. Since these water bodies are not easily accessible by land, recreation opportunities focus on the uplands. An extensive trail system takes hikers and horseback riders through scrub and flatwoods communities, habitats for numerous listed plants and animals. State Road 46, on the park's northern boundary, has two wildlife underpasses to help reduce the vehicle-caused deaths of the Florida black bear and smaller animals.

Rock Springs Run State Reserve is the most hydrologically diverse unit within the Wekiva River Basin State Parks having several springs and over 200 acres of depression marsh communities. These isolated wetlands range from small - less than three acres - round ponds, which resemble sinkhole lakes, to large marshy systems. During the droughts, many of the ponds dry completely.

Rock Springs Run is the Reserve's most distinctive feature. Its source is Rock Springs, located within Kelly Park, an Orange County recreation Park that is adjacent to Wekiwa Springs State Park. The average flow for Rock Springs is approximately 60 cubic feet a second, which equates to about 39 million gallons a day. From Kelly Park, the Run flows along a somewhat meandering eight miles before joining Wekiwa Springs Run to form the Wekiva River. Rock Springs Run forms a boundary between Wekiwa Springs State Park to the south and the Reserve to the north.

Several small-unnamed springs drain from the Reserve south into Rock Springs Run.

North of Shell Mound Road, an old borrow pit acts as an ephemeral wetland, holding water during wet periods. The pit has aquatic vegetation and several species of fish. Together, Hydric Hammock and Floodplain Swamp account for over 6,000 acres. Recent tram road removal projects have significantly enhanced the hydrology of many of these areas.

Note: The former town of Ethel's community cemetery lies within the park boundaries and has four intact grave markers (See History section).

Recreation Facilities

The reserve is managed according to the multiple-use concept which permits a variety of recreational activities considered to be compatible with the resources.

Trails
Hiking (14mi) • Equestrian (17mi) • Biking (15mi) • Multi-Use (32mi)

Primitive Camping
Canoe Access (2) - access from river only • Equestrian access (10)

Equestrian Facilities
Horse Barn

Restroom

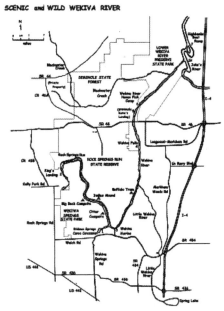

SCENIC and WILD WEKIVA RIVER

The reserve opens at 8 am and closes at sunset year-round.

Lower Wekiva River Preserve State Park

The Preserve borders two miles of the St. Johns River and the lower four miles of the Wekiva River and Black Water Creek. The preserve was purchased by the state of Florida in 1976 under the Environmentally Endangered Lands program, to protect portions of the lower Wekiva River while allowing limited recreational use.

The preserve has a variety of plant communities that maintain a high species diversity and biological richness. The unique black-water streams and associated wetlands provide habitat for a variety of rare and endangered animals.

Over 75 percent of the park is made up of wetland natural communities, primarily

Floodplain swamp and Hydric Hammock along the Wekiva and St. Johns River Basin. These communities depend on seasonal flood of the Wekiva and St. Johns Rivers. Other hydrologic features found include marshes, blackwater streams, and flatwoods lakes.

In the early to mid 1900s, several large tram roads were built within the northern sections of the park to facilitate the harvest of large cypress trees. In areas, these earthen roads are over 10 feet high and well over 20 feet wide.

The tram roads are actually spoil piles. Next to the roads are large ditches usually contain water. These tram roads significantly altered the hydrology of the areas. In 2002, approximately one mile of large tram roads was removed (a funded mitigation project). Between April and December of 2004, another one and one-half miles was removed. Culvert work was completed in 2004. Ditch blocks were placed in areas where it was not feasible to remove the tram roads, but these have been effective only in very low flow situations.

The Fecthal Tract north end has extensive areas of Flatwoods, Scrubby Flatwoods, and Scrub which are presently due to damaged culverts at several low water crossings

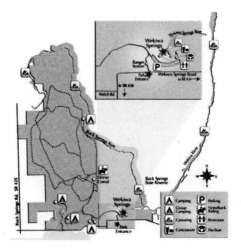

Canoeing and kayaking are the best way to view the magnificent wetland communities, the rivers, Black Water Creek and the wildlife. Katie's Landing, a recent addition to LWRPSP southeastern section, is the one place to access the river. It provides approximately 400 ft. of the Wekiva River's eastern shoreline, for launching canoes and kayaks.

There are hiking trails from the SR 46 entrance north along the eastern side of the Wekiva River. Included is a certified segment of the Florida National Scenic Trail. In the Ruderal areas on the northwestern side of the Preserve, hiking and equestrian activities may occur.

Recreation Facilities

Primitive Camping
Equestrian access (1)

Trails
Multi-Use (41mi)
The self-guided Sandhill Nature Trail provides a leisurely 50-minute walk.
Canoe (42mi)

Equestrian Facilities
Horse Barn
Restroom

Katie's Landing
Canoe/Kayak Launch

The park opens at 8 am and closes at sunset year-round.

Animals of Wekiwa Springs

Florida Black Bear (Ursus americanus floridanus)

Florida black bears are shy and rarely aggressive. They roam through the park and are most often seen at dusk. Average length is about 60 inches. The smaller females can grow up to 300 lbs while males can grow up to 400 lbs although the record is 624 lbs. The females (sows) have one to four cubs every two years. The breeding season is from June to August and the cubs are born in late January or early February. Bears are excellent climbers. Their diet is 80 percent plants, berries and nuts. When they do attack prey it is usually from ambush.

Note: Never approach or feed a bear. If you encounter one on the trail or around the campsite, slowly back away.

Status

Although the population of Florida black bears is drastically declining, the U.S. Fish and Wildlife Service has not listed them under the Endangered Species Act as threatened or endangered. However, they are listed as threatened by the state of Florida.

Description

These black bears often have a white band of fur across their chest. The distinct shape of their skull differs from those of other black bears. They are 4.5 to 6.5 feet long, making them larger than any other subspecies of black bears. Despite their size they can run up to 30 miles an hour and they are excellent climbers.

Population

It is estimated that there are between 1,500 and 2,500 Florida black bears.

Lifespan

Male bears usually live from 15-25 years, while females can live up to 30 years.

Range

Most of Florida's black bears occur in five major populations located in the Ocala/Wekiva River Basin, Big Cypress National Preserve, Apalachicola National Forest, Osceola National Forest and Eglin Air Force Base. A black bear will roam about 15 miles from its den and marks its territory by leaving claw marks on trees.

Habitat

Florida black bears can be found in a variety of habitats throughout Florida, including mixed hardwood pine, cabbage palm hammock, upland oak scrub, and forested wetlands, such as cypress and swamps.

Food

The Florida bear enjoys a wide variety of foods, including berries, acorns and fruits. They also eat insects, armadillos and carrion.

Behavior

Florida black bears do not truly hibernate. Late December to March, they have a period called "wintering" – a time when pregnant females give birth in the den and go without food. Males and non-pregnant females sometimes leave the den for short periods.

Offspring

Every two years in January or February, females give birth to two to four cubs. Their dens may be high in a tree, in a hollowed out stumps or on a forest floor protected by vegetation. Cubs are dependent on their mother's protection for nearly two years, during which time she fiercely protects them and teaches them lessons of survival.

Threats

The biggest long term threat facing the Florida black bear is loss of habitat as a result of development and urbanization. Vehicle-caused mortality (or "road kills") is the number one direct cause of death. Habitat fragmentation (highways built through bear habitat) can divide and isolate habitat areas bears need for food, water and shelter. Habitat fragmentation also makes it difficult for bears to find mates and limits their chances to move into more suitable habitat.

White tailed deer

Also known as the Virginia deer or whitetail, these animals stand about 30 inches at the shoulder and weigh between 72 and 125 lbs. Although shy, it is not unusual if you come across a deer on the trail that stands and stares at you. During the mating (rutting) season, between September and November, the bucks can be more aggressive. Only males have antlers which start to grow in late spring after the first year.

The deer's coat is a reddish-brown in the spring and summer and turns to a gray-brown throughout the fall and winter. The deer can be recognized by the characteristic white underside to its tail, which it shows as a signal of alarm by raising the tail during escape.

Deer, especially bucks, mark their territories by rubbing against trees. Bucks use their antlers to strip the bark off small trees. Females give birth to one or two, and very rarely three, fawns in May or early June.

Deer are ruminants which means they have four stomachs each of which performs a different digestive function. This allows them to eat a wide variety of food quickly and then digest it later when they are under cover.

Raccoon

An easy to spot animal because of its black eye patches, banded, bushy tail and unusual gait, the Florida raccoon grows to about 30 inches in length, smaller than its northern relatives. They are good swimmers and climbers and usually roam at night but may be out during the day. They like to live near water to moisten their food (frogs, fish, small mammals, birds, eggs and fruit) before eating. One explanation for this is that raccoons do not have very active salivary glands. Their dexterous hands allow them to open containers, backpacks and garbage cans. Raccoons live in hollow trees and have a litter of four of five young born in April or May. The young stay with their mother for about a year.

River Otter

These playful, intelligent semi-aquatic mammals can grow to 60 inches in length but are usually three to four feet long. Their tail makes up 30 to 40 percent of their body length. The males are larger than the females. Both have soft, dense, dark brown fur. While they prefer fish they will forage on land if necessary. They are graceful, agile swimmers and fast hunters on land. A male otter was timed running on land at 18 mph. They are most active at early morning and dusk. When swimming underwater the otter is able to close its nostrils. It can hold its breath for up to four minutes and during that time it can swim underwater up to a quarter of a mile.

Did you know? An otter can't swim when it is born, it has to be taught how to by its mother.

Sherman's Fox Squirrel

Being the largest member of the squirrel family, it grows to about 30 inches in length. It is easily recognized by its black face, white ears, large size and very long, bushy tail. It is so much bigger than the gray squirrel that some people mistake it for a monkey because of the way it sits erect on a tree branch. Although it is a tree squirrel it does feed on the ground, mostly on a diet of pine seeds, acorns, other nuts, fruits and insects. Its numbers are declining throughout the state.

Eastern Gray squirrel

If you hear rustling along the trail, it is probably a gray squirrel or a lizard. Excellent climbers and jumpers, gray squirrels are about 18-20 inches which includes an eight to 10 inch tail.

The tail has a number of purposes. It is often held over the squirrel's back to protect it from the heat and this is how it gets its name because the scientific name for the gray squirrel is "sciurus", the Greek word for shade. The tail can also be wrapped around the squirrel's body to provide warmth on cold days and it provides balance.

Bobcat

This ferocious fighter grows up to 36 inches and can weigh 25 lbs. It usually hunts for small prey in the early morning or late evening and is rarely seen. Although agile climbers, bobcats normally hunt on the ground. They spend their days sleeping in hollow logs or dense palmetto thickets. They are solitary creatures and only pair for breeding. Females rear the litter of two to three kittens.

Did you know? Bobcats are born with blue eyes but these change to brown as the cats mature.

Gray Fox

Gray foxes are confusing because they have quite a lot of red fur, especially on their sides, shoulders and undersides. Red foxes are more uniformly red and their tails have a distinctive white tip. They are not a native species and were originally introduced for hunting.

Gray foxes love forests and thick undergrowth where they are skilled night hunters. They grow to 36 inches in length but weigh only 20 to 22 lbs. Like the bobcat, they prefer to live in hollow logs. They are fast, have excellent sight, hearing and smell and are good climbers, often scaling trees when threatened. They often mate for life.

Armadillo

The nine-banded armadillo (which means "little armored one" in Spanish) is the only species of armadillo found in the United States. It is thought to have migrated from Texas to Florida about 150 years ago. Millions of years ago there were several species, the last of which became extinct about 10,000 years ago.

It is protected by nine hinged bands that overlap each other and provide its body armor.

They grow to 30 inches in length, have long tongues, powerful claws and are excellent diggers. If threatened one can dig a hole and bury itself in seconds.

They eat huge quantities of insects and they can smell an insect several inches underground. They live in burrows and feed mostly at night but sometimes forages during the day. While they have good eyesight and smell, they have very poor hearing. They are vulnerable because unlike other armadillos they cannot roll up into a complete ball thus their soft belly can be attacked. They are considered an exotic in Florida State Parks.

Among their many talents is their ability to cross bodies of water by holding their breath as they walks across the bottom. Females always give birth to identical quadruplets – either four males or four females.

Pocket gopher

You will probably never see one, but you can certainly spot where pocket gophers have been. Piles of sand are evidence of gopher burrowing. You can usually see their sand mounds around Sand Lake. This eight inch long rodent spends its entire life underground feeding on roots and tubers exposed while it burrows. It gets its name from the pockets or pouches on the outside of its cheeks. It uses the pouches to store food that it takes back to its burrow. The pocket gopher has the ability to close its lips behind its teeth. This allows it to use its teeth to tunnel without getting sand in its mouth.

Tunnels can be hundreds of feet long and there are two levels. The upper level is about one foot below the surface and is constantly being expanded as the pocket gopher forages for food. The lower level is where the pocket gopher hides when threatened and where it has its nest and rears its young.

Florida mouse

This five-seven inch long mouse with large ears is found only in Florida and is Florida's largest mouse. It is feeds at night and makes its home in gopher tortoise burrows which is why it is sometimes called the gopher mouse. It is listed as a species of special concern.

Opossum

These very adaptable tree living mammals venture to the ground at night to feed although you may see one during the day if it has been disturbed. They are about 30 inches from the tip of the pink nose to the end of the tail. The 12-inch hairless, prehensile tail is aids in climbing. If cornered they can be aggressive but prefer to run from a fight.

It is the only North American marsupial. A marsupial's young are born at an early stage of development and complete development in the mother's pouch. At birth they are so small that 20 could fit in one teaspoon. Usually 7 to 9 are born at a time. They spend about three months in the pouch and then cling to the mother's back as she forages for food. After another month they wander off to fend for themselves. Florida opossums usually have two litters a year.

Interesting fact: Opossums are immune to the poison of venomous snakes and have been known to kill Eastern diamondback rattlesnakes.

Florida Panther

Florida's state animal and one of the rarest and most endangered mammals in the world. It is one of about 30 subspecies that used to roam throughout South and North America. Its coat is darker and its hair stiffer than other subspecies and white flecks dot the back of the neck and shoulders. There is a cowlick (swirl of hair) in the middle of the back of the neck and the last three bones of its tail are bent giving it a crook at the end. Male panthers weigh up to 130 pounds, can be up to seven feet long and be up to 28 inches high at the shoulders. Adult females are smaller and usually weigh between 60 and 80 pounds.

Today they are restricted to deserts, tropical rain forests, mountains and other areas having little human encroachment. Florida panthers are found mainly in the Everglades and Big Cypress regions of south Florida although they have been seen in counties around Wekiwa. Their territories range from 40 to more than 200 square miles. In hot weather they generally travel at night. They are solitary animals and usually only range together when mating,

While rarely seen, panthers can travel up to 20 miles in a day, but tend to stay in an area for several days after a kill. Prey is mainly deer and hogs, but they will take smaller animals such as armadillos. A female has between two and four kittens in a litter.

It is not known how many Florida panthers exist. Estimates range from 50 to 90. They have no natural enemies, but are threatened by destruction of habitat and motor vehicles.

Coyote

Having exceptional hearing, sight and smell they are very efficient hunters, mostly of small mammals and birds, but have been known to take deer. They have reddish, gray fur and look like German Shepherds with shorter legs. Coyotes are making a comeback in the Florida peninsula because of their ability to survive in almost any kind of habitat

Manatee

These massive, gentle beasts were once so common in the Wekiva River that it was difficult for boatmen to maneuver. Today, manatees are rarely seen in the Wekiva preferring to winter in warmer waters like estuaries and Blue Springs State Park. When they venture into the Wekiva River they are encouraged to swim back to the St. Johns River.

Manatees are gray with strong, front flippers and a broad tail. They have a thick cleft upper lip which is used to grasp food, and bristles on their lips which help guide food into their mouths.

They often use their flippers to hold food. They feed on a wide variety aquatic plants that wear their teeth down. But new teeth, produced at the back of the mouths, are constantly replacing worn teeth. As front teeth wear down, new teeth move up to replace them.

They swim slowly and often rest on the bottom. They have to come to the surface to breathe, but can remain submerged for up to 15 minutes.

Manatees are docile creatures and have no natural predators. They can grow up to 13 feet long and weigh 1,500lbs. - one was weighed at 3,500lbs. They can live to 60 years in the wild. The female has a single calf which is born underwater. Boat propellers pose one of their greatest hazards.

Bats

There are several species of bats in the parks and all are insect eaters. Bats are the only mammals that can fly. While flying they use echolocation to locate prey. The

Northern Yellow Bat is one of the state's largest bats. It is solitary, has a length of four to five inches, and yet weighs less than an ounce. During the day they like to roost in clumps of Spanish moss hanging from trees. Often they leave their roosts before dark and thus are the species most likely to be seen at dusk.

The Evening Bat emerges well after dusk from its roost in or close to cypress stands.

Rafinesque's Big-Eared Bat has the largest ears of all Florida's bats. When roosting the ears are folded back under the wings. The Seminole bat has a 12- inch wingspan and nests low to the ground preferring to roost in Spanish moss dangling from tree limbs.

Bird Life

Wekiwa Springs has a fantastic birdlife with more than 163 species recorded – more than half the total number of species recorded in Florida. Woodpeckers, red bellied, red headed and pileated (the largest) are probably seen most often in the woods. The undergrowth teems with tiny warblers that are difficult to spot and even harder to identify. Look for the Florida scrub-jay in Oak Scrub and Scrubby Flatwoods. You can't miss the red-winged blackbird or the striking all-red male cardinal.

Overhead are birds of prey such as osprey, bald eagle, American kestrel, red shouldered hawk and swallow tailed kite and vultures. The waters are host to a wealth of duck, waders and water birds such as herons, egrets and ibis. You can see wood storks and look out for limpkins, a member of the crane family. The limpkin, a 24 inch tall wading bird common only in Florida's peninsula feeds, on apple snails, frogs and small lizards.

Florida Scrub Jay

The Florida scrub jay differs from the blue jay in that it lacks a crest and white wing markings and its back is gray-brown instead of blue. Florida scrub jays are declining because their habitat is disappearing.

Pairs usually mate for life and rarely leave their dry scrub territory. Young also stay and often help their parents feed later broods and defend the family territory.

Scrub jays like low, dense thickets where they can nest, next to large open areas, where they can feed on insects, snakes, spiders and lizards. They also eat berries and acorns that like squirrels they bury to provide food during the winter. Fire is important to their habitat because scrub jays need clear open spaces to feed.

Bald Eagles

These protected and magnificent birds with a wing span of over seven feet, are easily recognized by their white head and tail, dark body and large, hooked bill. However, head and tail do not turn white until four years of age. They are predominately fish eaters, but will eat reptiles, water birds and carrion.

Bald eagles mate for life and build a large nest, or refurbish an old one, in the fall and early winter. Nests are usually high in tall pine trees. After many years nests often get so large and heavy that they topple to the ground. Two eggs are laid and then incubated by both parents for around 35 days. The young fledge in 10 to 12 weeks. While the number of bald eagles has dropped significantly in the last 50 years, the population now seems to have stabilized with Florida one of the main breeding areas in the U.S.

Wild Turkeys

Common throughout the parks these are the largest game bird in North America. Males can be four feet tall and females three feet. In the spring males, called toms or gobblers, strut around with the wings trailing on the ground and their large tails fanned out to attract females (hens). The males are called gobblers because of the noise they make which can be heard up to a quarter of a mile away. They roost in trees at night.

Peregrin Falcon

Also called the duck hawk, it is the world's fastest bird. It can reach speeds of 75 mph when swooping on prey – other birds in flight. It circles high in the sky until it spots a prey and then dives on it. It either catches a prey in mid-air or knocks it out of the air and then kills it on the ground.

Once common throughout North and South America, it is now a rare breeding species east of the Mississippi.

American Swallow-Tailed Kite

This is a spectacular black and white bird of prey that effortlessly soars high in the sky. They spend the fall and winter in South America and arrive in Florida in early March to breed. They build nests of small sticks woven with Spanish moss, preferably in tall cypress and pine. These trees emerge from a canopy of prey-rich woodlands, like those of swamps and savannas. Highly social for a raptor, they nest in loose colonies and often forage in small flocks. Once common throughout southeastern US they are now mostly found in Florida.

They eat all kinds of insects and small animals, including frogs, anoles and snakes. By early July, they begin to gather in large communal roosts for the migration back to South America.

Anhinga

The Anhinga, also known as the snake bird because of its long neck, is a resident species that feeds on fish, shrimp, small amphibians, baby alligators and snakes. Anhingas lack the oil glands that most other aquatic birds possess, so you can often spot them perched on a branch with wings outstretched, drying their feathers. The lack of oil enables the feathers to become waterlogged so the bird can swim better underwater.

Good Bird Watching Areas

Sand Lake for northern bobwhite, woodpeckers, eastern bluebird, flycatchers and red winged blackbirds.

Lake Prevatt for ducks, ospreys and eagles.

Uplands plays host to migrant species wintering in the park - yellow rumped warbler, oven birds, palm warbler, ruby crowned kinglets, cedar waxwings, and eastern phoebes. Bald eagles can usually be seen from October to March.

Reptiles and Amphibians

Florida boasts 60 species of snakes, 25 species of lizards, 57 species of amphibians and countless species of insects. Not all of these, however, are found in the Wekiwa River Basin State Parks. The most famous of Florida's reptiles is, of course, the alligator and there are lots of them in Wekiwa Springs State Park. The alligator is also Florida's State Reptile.

Florida's amphibians are split into two main groups: (1) salamanders, anoles, skinks and newts and (2) frogs and toads. Most live in or near water and depend on it to provide moisture as they lose water through their thin, moist skins.

Toads and skinks have thicker skins so do better in dryer habitats. Amphibians are mostly active at night or during rainy weather in order to maintain body moisture. Anoles, often mistakenly called chameleons, are able to change their color to blend into their surroundings.

Florida has 24 species of frogs and two species of toads. The Florida chorus frog, so named because it loves to sing day and night, is only one inch long while the southern bullfrog can grow to seven inches. It takes more than a year for a bullfrog to change from a tadpole into a frog. Each species of frog and toad has its own distinct call and they are especially vocal during mating time which, in Florida, runs from April to September.

Alligators

Although plentiful, 'gators are protected because they are similar in appearance to the endangered American crocodiles. Gators have a wider skull than crocodiles and their fourth tooth protrudes. Males can grow to 14 feet, and females 10 feet. The largest alligator caught in Florida was 14 feet and 1/8 inch.

An adult gator's brain is the size of a dime so pretty much everything is done by instinct. An alligator' eye has three eyelids – upper and lower ones that close to cut out vision and a transparent one that moves sideways across the eye when underwater. This eyelid protects the eye from water but allows the gator to spot prey. When swimming the legs are tucked in against its body and it propels itself moving its strong tail side to side.

There are sensors on the jaws that detect movement in the water. The jaws exert 2-3,000 lbs of pressure per square inch when biting - human jaws exert 5 lb of pressure when biting full force. Most of the jaw muscle power is for shutting the mouth. The opening muscles are not very strong, thus alligator wrestlers can clamp their hands around the end of the gator's snout and prevent it from opening its jaws.

A gator's diet is 80% fish but it will eat turtles, mammals, snakes, birds, other alligators and carrion. They generally don't eat if the water temperature falls below 70 degrees. Gators have blunt stubby teeth used to grip prey that is then swallowed whole. Throughout its lifetime, new teeth grow and replace old worn ones.

In June or July, females make mounds of vegetation, close to water, in which they lay 30-50 eggs. The embryo breathes through a dry spot in the shell. If an egg is moved the dry spot may be covered, thus suffocating the embryo.

A nest's temperature determines the sex of the hatchlings. If the temperature is hot (90-93°F), males are produced; if it is warm (82-86°F), females emerge from the eggs. If the temperature is between the two, roughly half will be male and half female. The mother does not move far from the nest during incubation and usually lies with her head over the eggs.

Hatching occurs when the shell is broken down by the combination of carbonic acid, created from carbon dioxide exhaled by the embryo, and water. Gators grow about eight or nine inches a year for their first few years, so a three-foot gator is probably four to five years old. Older gators stop growing longer and tend to grow wider. Gators can live to 40 years in the wild.

A male gator protects a territory of about 20 acres while a female's territory is usually around five acres. They are found in both natural and man-made freshwater lakes, ponds, rivers and wet areas. They are most active at night. If you shine a flash-light over a pond or lake at night, you can pick out gators by their red eyes staring back at you.

Alligators have been found to have an unusually strong immune system that can fight off types of bacteria, viruses and fungi without having been exposed to them previously, thus protecting them from a wide range of infections. According to Lan-cia Darville, a Louisiana State University researcher, who is studying alligator blood, it contains many special proteins that provide infection protection. She said: "If you think about alligators, they usually get into a lot of fights and get cuts and bruises and torn limbs, and they live in swamps that have a whole lot of bacteria. But even in the presence of all that bacteria, they almost never get any infections."

The Gator's eggs contain natural interferon – an effective cancer fighting drug that is produced in the uterus during egg production.

The American Alligator has been Florida's State Reptile since 1987.

Did You Know? You can tell the length of a gator even if you can only see its head above water. The length from the nose flares to the eyes in inches is the length of the gator in feet.

Gopher Tortoise

The gopher tortoise (**gopherus polyphemus**) belongs to a group of land tortoises that originated in North America 60 million years ago, thus making it one of the oldest living species. They are either a dark tan, or gray. Their front legs are broad and flat, almost like a shovel. The top part of the shell is fairly flat. The adult gopher tortoise is a rather drab looking animal in contrast to the brightly colored hatchlings.

They grow to an average length of slightly less than a foot and weight of about 29 pounds. They have been found to be as long as 16 inches. They can live to 100 years. These gentle land creatures are found throughout Florida and southern areas of Georgia, South Carolina, Mississippi, Alabama and the tip of Eastern Louisiana.

Gopher tortoises dig burrows in dry, well-drained soil having lots of vegetation for food. The burrow provides protection from predators, the elements and from extreme conditions such as droughts, freezing weather, and fires. Burrows can be as short as 6 to 10 feet, but average about 30 feet. The longest found is approximately 50 ft. Depths vary from 3 to 20 feet - often limited by the ground water level. The burrows vary in shape, but most are straight or have slight curves. The burrow's entrance is just large enough for the tortoise that excavated it. The top of the entrance is curved so the carapace can just get through.

Feeding during the day, they graze on vegetation just like cows, and thus, are important players in spreading seeds. They are primarily herbivores feeding on many species of low-growing plants. Their diet is largely grasses and legumes. They also eat gopher apple, pawpaw, blackberries, saw palmetto berries, and other fruits and will scavenge. They are opportunistic feeders, occasionally feeding on dead animals and excrement.

Gopher tortoises rarely drink (or are rarely seen drinking). They can use their front flipper like legs to dam-up rain water running into a burrow. Most of the water they get comes from food. During periods of extreme drought they have been seen drinking standing water.

The gopher tortoise reaches sexual maturity between 12 and 15 years of age, when its shell is about 9 inches long. It has an elaborate courtship that begins in the spring. It nests between April and July. Typically, a nest is about six inches deep, close to the burrow opening so the sun can warm the soil and incubate the eggs. A clutch of 4 to 7 round ping-pong ball size eggs is laid.

The young hatch in about 80 to 90 days and often spend the first winter in their mother's burrow, although they have to fend for themselves. Hatchlings are 1 to 2 inches long and grow about 3/4 inch a year. The temperature of the sand or dirt of the nest determines the sex of the offspring. If the temperature is above 30° C (85° F), the tortoise's hatchling will be females. Temperatures below 30° C produce males.

When determining the sex of a tortoise, the most noticeable difference is that the male's plastron (bottom part of shell) is concave whereas, the female's is perfectly flat.

Ecosystem Importance

The gopher tortoise is a very important part of the local ecology. As in any food web, removing certain flora or fauna, can adversely affect the survival of the ecosystem. The gopher tortoise is especially important because their burrows provide homes for other animals. About 250 species of animals at one time or another use the burrows, including: indigo and other snakes, gopher frogs, mice, foxes, skunks, opossums, rabbits, quail, armadillos, burrowing owls, lizards, frogs, toads and other invertebrates. Some species share the burrows with the tortoises and others utilize abandoned burrows. Thus, removing the tortoises from the local habitat leaves many animals without homes. Some animals are able to relocate, but a few species are only found in these burrows.

The Florida gopher tortoise is on the Endangered Species List, categorized as a Species of Special Concern. This means that the population is decreasing, but how much is not known. Several studies are being conducted to determine the population and how it is changing.

Loss of habitat is the primary reason for being endangered, but in the past many tortoises were killed for food, and as an effort to kill rattlesnakes that shared the burrows. Gopher tortoises are now contracting, and being killed by, a contagious infection called Upper Respiratory Tract Disease.

We can help gopher tortoises in the wild by preserving their upland habitats. If you see a tortoise, or turtle trying to cross a road, help it safely across without changing the direction in which it is traveling. Never transport a tortoise out of its habitat - one sick tortoise can infect an entire population of healthy ones.

Turtles

The park is home to many species of turtle including the aggressive common snapping turtle. Other species include the Florida box turtle, Common Cooter, Florida chicken turtle, Florida mud turtle, Florida redbelly turtle, loggerhead musk turtle, painted turtle and the aptly-named. stinkpot, a small turtle that emits a dreadful odor when threatened.

Turtles can live 30 to 40 years in the wild.

Eastern Box Turtle

Terrapene carolina carolina

Box turtles are probably the best known of all the turtle species. Several varieties live in the United States. The Eastern Box Turtle is native to the southern Appalachian Mountains.

Description

The high-domed shell is the most prominent feature of the box turtle. The lower shell (plastron) is hinged, enabling the shell to close much like a box. The upper shell (carapace) and the plastron, are typically dark brown to black with many varying streaks, spots, and lines of yellow and orange. Older turtles often have very smooth and worn shells with little coloration. The head, neck, and legs of box turtles are also brightly colored with yellow and orange, particularly in the males.

A male's eyes are usually bright red or orange while a female's eyes are usually dark red or brown. A male box turtle has a slight depression in the middle of its lower shell while a female's lower shell is flat.

Adults are typically 5 to 6 inches. In the wild they typically live 30 to 40 years and some are believed to have reached 100.

Habits and Habitats

Box turtles are found from fields to forests, but seem to prefer moist areas when available. During hot, dry weather, box turtles often seek springs and seepages where they dig deeply into the cool mud. When emerging to feed, they spend much time buried in leaves and dirt on the forest floor, especially after or during rainstorms. They eat many kinds of plant and animal material including berries, mushrooms, earthworms, slugs, snails, and insects.

Like other reptiles, they hibernate during cold winter weather. In October they burrow deep under the soil and leaves, usually emerging in April or early May.

When disturbed or frightened, a box turtle will generally pull its head and legs in and tightly close its shell until the threat passes. The shell is extremely tough and almost impossible to pry open. Box turtles do not develop the hinge for closing the shell until they are 4 to 5 years old.

Females seek sunny warm soil areas to lay their eggs. They excavate holes with their hind feet. Although box turtles are active during daylight hours, females often use the protective cover of darkness to lay eggs. After laying from 3 to 6 eggs, the nest is covered with soil and the eggs left to hatch.

Box turtles usually lay their eggs in western North Carolina in June and July. Hatching occurs 2 to 3 months later. Sometimes turtles hatch late and may winter in the nest, emerging the following spring. Due to their small size and lack of the bright coloration young box turtles are seldom seen.

History

While common in many areas, box turtles have declined over much of their range, probably largely due to habitat destruction by man. Many box turtles are killed crossing roads. Dogs sometimes catch box turtles and chew their shells, resulting in injury and eventual death to the turtles. Hiding in tall grass, many are hit by lawn mowers. They are popular pets and over collecting for the pet trade can seriously reduce their numbers. In spite of threats, box turtles can often survive close to man in suitable pockets of habitat.

Because of its popularity and well-known status, the Eastern Box Turtle was chosen as North Carolina's official state reptile in 1979.

Snakes

Of the 27 species of snake found in the park, only four are venomous - the pygmy rattlesnake, eastern diamondback rattlesnake, water moccasin (cottonmouth) and eastern coral snake. Contrary to popular belief, snakes are not aggressive and will usually only attack if cornered or surprised. While they like to laze in the sun on a path, they will normally slither away when they hear you approach. They usually live in holes so NEVER put your hand in a hole.

The **water moccasin** has the reputation of being the most aggressive snake and while it will threaten an attack, it rarely strikes even when harassed because its venom is too valuable to waste on 'non food'. When threatened, it may open its mouth wide revealing the whitish inner lining (thus its name cottonmouth) - much as a rattlesnake vibrate its tail shaking its rattle These are warnings to back off.

Water moccasins like to sun bathe on land and on logs near the water. When swimming they hold their heads above water. They are not good climbers, thus stories about their falling off branches into canoes are probably not true. Non-venomous water snakes, are agile climbers that like to bask on tree limbs overhanging water. It is these that have probably lost their grips and ended up as uninvited guests in canoes.

Eastern diamondback rattlesnakes are dangerous because of their size (up to seven feet long), the amount of venom they can deliver and their rapid striking speed. It is easily identified by its yellow-bordered diamond shaped markings and arrow shaped head that is much larger than its neck. Most commonly found in palmetto flatlands, pine woods and brushy and grassy areas, although it is very difficult to see because its color pattern blends in so well with its background.

The rattlesnake does not have to be coiled to strike but when coiled it can strike over a distance equivalent to half its body length or more. It can strike three or four times, each time returning to its coiled position, in less than two seconds. When it is agitated the snake will vibrate its rattle which can be heard up to 400 yards away. Rattlesnakes shed their skins up to five times a year - depending on how much food has been available and, thus how much they have grown.

The **pygmy rattlesnake** is also common throughout Florida and its rattle produces a buzzing sound that cannot be heard more than a few feet away. Most are less than 18 inches long. Like other pit vipers, the pygmy rattlesnake does not lay eggs but gives live birth to its young. Its bite is painful and one should be medically treated, but there is no known case of a pygmy rattlesnake bite having been fatal to a human.

Of the park's listed species the largest snake in the park is the slate-blue **eastern indigo snake** that can grow to 8 feet. When the snakes emerge from the eggs they can be up to 24 inches long. They can grow to 48 inches in the first year. They prefer dry pinelands and moist subtropical hammocks. They feed during the cooler parts of the day (early morning and late afternoon) on small mammals, birds, amphibians and other snakes. They rest during the hottest part of the day, usually in gopher tortoise burrows.

Many species of snake can be confused with others. Non-venomous water snakes are often confused with water moccasins. The non-venomous **kingsnake**, is often confused with the highly venomous **coral snake** - both have red, black and yellow bands. The easiest way to tell them apart is that the coral snake has a black snout and the kingsnake has a red one. Also there is the rhyme: "red touch yellow, kill a fellow; red touch black, good for Jack".

The coral snake is a shy and secretive snake, rarely more than two feet long that likes rotting logs and piles of decaying vegetation. Its venom is the most potent of any North American snake. It bites and chews its prey to drive its small fangs in before releasing venom.

Did You Know?

Venom remains toxic even after a snake dies. A man who cut off the head of a rattlesnake was bitten when he bent down to pick it up. A Washington state Fish and Wildlife Department biologist said it's possible the snake had the heat-sensing ability to make one last attack or it may have been a reflex.

Spiders and Scorpions

Spiders are plentiful in the parks and although all can bite, only two are dangerous – the brown recluse and the black widow. Seek medical attention if bitten by either of these spiders. The brown recluse is the most dangerous because its venom breaks down human tissue and no antivenin has yet been developed. Without quick medical attention after a bite, flesh around the bite will die and the wound will get larger and larger as more and more tissue is irreversibly destroyed.

The black widow's venom is dangerous – up to 20 times more potent than a rattlesnake's venom - but there are antivenins. However, there are few fatalities because when a black widow bites it generally does not release much venom. The black widow is easily identified by its shiny black body and the red hourglass shape on its abdomen

Not all Florida's spiders weave webs. The wolf spider senses movement, leaps on its prey and disables it with its long fangs. A disturbed wolf spider will bite a human but its bite, while painful, is not fatal.

Orb weavers are large, long legged spiders that weave large webs. The female sits in the center of the web waiting for prey. Golden-silk orbweavers are as large as your hand and like to weave webs across paths, four to five feet off the ground, so be alert when hiking,

Florida scorpions are small and rarely more than 3 inches long. They are found throughout Florida. They hide during the day in rotting wood and under rocks. Its stinger, in the arched tail end, delivers a nasty sting but it is not serious unless one suffers an allergic reaction. The female gives birth to live young which she then carries on her back for several days before they go off to fend for themselves. Scorpions have remained almost unchanged for hundreds of millions of years.

Insects

There are tens of thousands of species found in the state, at least 500 of which are found only in Florida, and scientists continue to discover new species. Some insects are friendlier than others.

There are wonderful butterflies (like the spectacular monarch and swallowtails), dragonflies, mayflies, damselflies, centipedes, grasshoppers, crickets, cicadas and beetles. Still fascinating but not so friendly are hornets, yellowjackets, wasps and bees, all of which can sting. Hornets, wasps and yellowjackets live in colonies. If you see a lot of these insects, it is best to move away, as you may be near a nest. There are the aptly-named stink bugs, the Hercules beetle (Florida's largest) and the bombardier beetle. The later can propel a spray of deadly chemicals from its abdomen at enemies.

Ants, especially fire ants, can give nasty bites, so it is best to inspect for ants before sitting on the ground. Florida carpenter ants can be half an inch long. Fire ants mate in flight. The female lands to lay eggs and start a new colony. A colony may eventually have a population of more than 250,000.

Mosquitoes, more than just pests, can spread life threatening diseases such as encephalitis and West Nile virus at certain times of year.

Ticks, chiggers and mites can latch on to you when walking trails. Ticks and chiggers can spread diseases and mites burrow under the skin, so inspect for them and remove unwelcome guests as quickly as possible. Sand fleas can also be a pest.

Fish

Florida has about 1,000 species of saltwater fish and around 230 species of freshwater fish. The rivers and lakes in the parks support a rich fish population including largemouth bass, bluegill, Florida gar, longnose gar, swamp darter, pirate perch, chain pickerel, snail bullhead and striped mullet. The gar thrives in low-oxygenated water because it has a swim bladder that attaches to its esophagus that acts like a lung. The gar surfaces and gulps air allowing it to survive in low-oxygenated waters when other fish cannot. Bluegills are part of the Sunfish family, a species found only in North America. They are a member of the bream genus.

Did You Know?
Catfish have a slime on their body which contains at least 60 proteins known to aid healing wounds in humans. Scientists are now investigating.

Plants

Florida has more tree species than any other state in the United States. Because of the state's temperate and sub tropical climates, it is home to more than 300 tree species, almost half the total species found in the U.S.

There are seven species of pine, 11 species of palm and more than 25 species of oak, some of them huge trees and others no larger than small bushes. Bald Cypress trees, named because they drop their needles in early spring, can grow for thousands of years and have enormous diameters although annual growth is very small. Water loving red maples are plentiful in the parks' Floodplain Swamps and Hydric Hammocks. There are also hundreds of species of wildflowers and other plants to be found in the parks.

There are flowering vines, air plants, the beautiful yet poisonous lantana, an exotic, and the white flowers of the buttonbush.

Resurrection ferns are found on the boughs of live oaks and other old trees. The ferns get their name because they almost disappear in dry weather then burst into life again after rain. Oaks are host to all sorts of other plants such as orchids, Virginia creeper, wild grapes, lichens, air plants and mosses, including Spanish moss – gathered by early settlers for stuffing pillows and mattresses.

A greater variety of trees, shrubs and flowers live in the parks than almost anywhere else in Florida. There are many different habitats, each supporting its own flora and fauna. For more information about habitats and their flora, see the Habitat Section above.

Endangered, Threatened and Species of Special Concern

The Endangered Species Act was passed by the U.S. Congress in 1973 and today, provides protection for more than 1,300 species of wildlife and plants worldwide. There are five main reasons why species become endangered – loss of habitat, disease or predation, over utilization, lack of regulations or enforcement, and other natural or man-made factors.

An **endangered species** is one that is or soon may be in immediate danger of extinction unless the species or its habitat is fully protected and managed for its survival.

A **threatened species** is one that is very likely to become endangered in the very near future unless the species or its habitat is fully protected and managed for its survival.

A **species of special concern** is one that warrants special protection because it may, due to pending degradation or human disturbance, become threatened.

Designated species are those that are listed by the Florida Natural Areas Inventory (FNAI), U.S. Fish and Wildlife Service (USFWS), Florida Fish and Wildlife Conservation Commission (FFWCC), and/or the Florida Department of Agriculture and Consumer Services (FDA) as endangered, threatened or of special concern.

There are currently 73 designated plant (23) and animal (50) species found in the WRBSP. This high number of species is a reflection of the biologically diverse nature of the basin.

Plants

There are 23 designated plants within the parks. The following is a discussion on one endangered species: star anise (*Illicium parviflorum*), and three other sensitive species: hand fern (*Ophioglossum palmatum*), the butterfly orchid (*Encyclia tampensis*) and the hooded pitcher plant (*Sarracenia minor*).

In addition to the designated plants, the Wekiva River Basin State Parks has a number of plants species considered distinctive. None is currently listed as designated species, nor are they rare or on the decline, but their presence in the Wekiva Basin is considered unusual. Many of these plants have distributions, which are more closely tied to the Appalachian Mountains than to Central Florida. Some of the occurrences represent southern or near southern range limits while others are disjunct populations. These distinctive species include red buckeye (*Aesculus pavia*), Florida leucothoe (*Agarista populifolia*), hornbeam (*Carpinus carolineana*), chinquapin (*Castanea alnifolia*), flowering dogwood (*Cornus florida*), witch hazel (*Hamamelis virginiana*), tulip poplar (*Liriodendron tulipifera*), wafer ash (*Ptelea trifoliata*), Carolina basswood (*Tilia caroliniana*), and poison sumac (*Toxicodendron vernix*).

Star anise (*Illicium parviflorum*). Wekiwa Springs State Park has the distinction of having the state's largest recognized population of star anise. Star anise occurs throughout the Hydric Hammock/Floodplain Swamp communities along Rock Springs Run. The plant was particularly abundant along the hiking trail that runs from Sand Lake to Camp Cozy. The Nature Conservancy registered the park in their habitat conservation program, recognizing the park's significance to this rare plant. One large population of star anise was secondarily impacted by logging that occurred to ameliorate the affects of the Southern pine beetles.

Hand fern (*Ophioglossum palmatum*). These are known to grow only in the bootjacks of cabbage palm petioles. The fern prefers areas near streams with high humidity and heavy shading. Hand ferns are very sensitive to fire, since the community in which they live rarely experiences fire. They are also very sensitive to reduced canopy cover resulting in lower relative humidity and increased sunlight.

Butterfly orchid (*Encyclia tampensis*). Over the past several years, volunteers have been regularly monitoring several populations of butterfly orchids. Several of these orchids were transplanted from Tosohatchee State Reserve to Wekiwa Springs State Park.

Hooded pitcher plant (*Sarracenia minor*). A number of small isolated populations are known throughout the Wekiva River Basin State Parks.

Animals and Birds

There are 50 designated animals within the parks. Discussion here will be limited to three endemic invertebrates: Wekiwa hydrobe (*Aphaostracon monas*), Wekiwa siltsnail (*Cincinnatia wekiwae*), blue purse-web spider (*Sphodros abboti*) and Orlando cave crayfish (*Procambarus acherontis*); three threatened species: Florida black bear (*Ursus americanus floridanus*), Florida scrub-jay (*Aphelocoma coerulescens*), and

Florida mouse (*Podomys floridanus*); two species of special concern: gopher tortoise (*Gopherus polyphemus*) and Florida gopher frog (*Rana capito aesopus*); and two other sensitive species: American swallow-tailed kite (*Elanoides forficatus*) and the striped newt (*Notophthalmus perstriatus*).

Wekiwa hydrobe (*Aphaostracon monas*) / **Wekiwa siltsnail** (*Cincinnatia wekiwae*). These two invertebrates were discovered in and near the WSSP main spring area in the 1970s. They were found on vegetation and in sand in the spring boil, and in the very upper reaches of the Spring-run. Vegetation is seasonally limited in the spring boil; however, there is still some year-round vegetation near the bridge area where the boil enters the lagoon area.

Orlando cave crayfish (*Procambarus acherontis*). This invertebrate is restricted to groundwater sites associated with six or seven spring cave systems of the lower Wekiva River Basin. Within the Wekiva River Basin State Parks, this species has only been recorded as found in WSSP. This species is a candidate for listing by the United States Fish and Wildlife Service.

Blue purse-web spider (*Sphodros abboti*). This rare species spins a bizarre tube-like web at the base of trees in Mesic woods. It was discovered in WSSP by park staff and confirmed by a Florida Fish and Wildlife Conservation Commission employee in 2002. This is the southernmost range limit for this species, extending its previously recognized distribution from the Ocala National Forest into the Wekiva Basin.

Florida gopher frog (*Rana capito aesopus*). The gopher frog uses gopher tortoise burrows. This amphibian is state listed. Its greatest threat is loss of habitat.

Striped newt (*Notophthalmus perstriatus*). A unique southern population of striped newt occurs within one known wetland of RSRSR. Of special interest is that this is one of two extant populations known within the southern range limits for this species.

Gopher tortoise (*Gopherus polyphemus*). The gopher tortoise, located throughout the WRBSP, is a "keystone" species because many other species, including a number of listed species, use the gopher tortoise burrows. The gopher tortoise is susceptible to upper respiratory tract disease

American swallow-tailed kite (*Elanoides forficatus*). This species occurs throughout the Wekiva River Basin State Parks.

Florida scrub-jay. Another designated species, the Florida scrub-jay (FSJ) is endemic to Florida and exclusively uses oak scrub and scrubby flatwoods communities. It has historic populations in all three parks of the Wekiva River Basin State

Parks. Currently it appears that the RSRSR population is declining rapidly and significantly.

The closest relative (Western scrub-jay, *A. californica*) is located in the western United States. Both species have adapted to similar harsh dry natural communities, developing complex social structures to benefit their survivals. The FSJ are cooperative breeding birds, occupying a single territory with all siblings acting as a family unit. The FSJ has a relatively narrow tolerance of scrub oak height and density. Successful nest building only occurs within that range. Once vegetation height and density becomes unsuitable, the jay's reproductive success declines but all the birds rarely completely abandon even unsuitable sites.

Florida mouse (*Podomys floridanus*). Like the Florida gopher frog, the Florida mouse is a highly specialized Florida endemic that uses tortoise burrows. It has one of the narrowest habitat ranges of any Florida mammal but is found throughout the basin parks.

Florida black bear (*Ursus americanus floridanus*). The Florida black bear is the most prominent of the designated species in the Wekiva Basin. They occur throughout the basin. The black bear, a flagship species, has led the charge for multi-agency land acquisition programs in the basin to secure connectivity to source populations in the Ocala National Forest. Wekiva bears are within the southern range limits of the Ocala /St. Johns population, one of six major Florida population areas. Previous radio tracking work conducted within the Wekiva Basin has suggested that bear densities are higher in this region than in any other parts of the State. Unfortunately, roads cutting through the Wekiva Basin experience the highest vehicle caused bear mortality rate in the State.

Exotic Species

Exotic species are plants and animals that are not native to Florida, but were introduced by human-related activities. Exotics have fewer natural enemies and may have higher survival rates than do native species, as well. They may also harbor diseases or parasites that significantly affect non-resistant native species. Consequently, it is the strategy to remove exotic species from native natural communities.

Most exotic plants within the WRBSP are not species that threaten to create monocultures (e.g. Brazilian pepper, melaleuca) but are instead persistent and widespread species that tend to encroach upon, but not exclude, native species. Some aquatic exotic plants are forming monocultures and out-competing native species in large areas. Most of the exotic plants are species that have escaped from cultivation. All the exotics are a threat to the integrity of the basin's natural communities and conflict with the Division of Recreation and Parks' goal of preserving and maintaining examples of the natural Florida.

Plants

Hydrilla (*Hydrilla verticillata*) occurs only within Wekiwa Springs State Park. In 2002 and 2004, the lagoon was severely choked with hydrilla. The noxious plant covered approximately 90 percent of the lagoon's surface. Chemicals were successfully used to treat the infestation.

Wild taro (*Colocasia esculenta*) is native to the Pacific Islands, and sold as an ornamental because of its large leaves. Wild taro is found within WSSP, throughout Rock Springs Run and along the Wekiva River. It is a very serious exotic problem plant impacting freshwater marshes and streams by covering water surfaces and shading out native plants. It grows quickly, reproduces by seeds and stolons and spreads by pieces of plants breaking off and floating downstream. It is found as scattered plants, as dense floating mats and as dense rooted clumps. Rock Springs Run and the Little Wekiva River are sources of infestation to the entire Wekiva River. The dense infestations require chemical treatment.

(*Eichhornia crassipes*) is native to Central and South America. It oc-
iwa State Park in several places along Rock Springs Run and within
It occurs in relatively low concentrations but forms very large
imes block boat traffic along the river. This species

Water lettuce (*Pistia stratiotes*) occurs in the lagoon area within WSSP and along both Rock Springs Run and the Wekiva River. The lettuce forms dense mats in areas where water flow is minimal.

Water-cress (*Nasturtium* sp.) has escaped from cultivation and occurs in small amounts in Rock Springs Run.

Pampas grass (*Cortederia selloana*). Has been found growing in several clumps on the sandbars in the flats area near the river cabin on Rock Springs Run.

Bamboo (*Bambusa* sp.) is native of China and there are two known remaining stands within Wekiva River Basin State Parks. Bamboo is a persistent exotic, but it spreads very slowly.

Air-potato (*Dioscorea bulbifera*) is a native to tropical Asia that escaped from cultivation. It occurs in disturbed woods and thickets in scattered locations. Under the right conditions, this vine is very prolific and becomes dense enough to shade out native species.

The **camphor tree** is native to Asia and occurs widely within Wekiwa River Basin State Parks.

Chinese wisteria (*Wisteria sinensis*) has historically been found in the main spring-head area of Wekiwa Springs State Park.

Chinaberry (*Melia azedarach*) is native of Asia, often used as an ornamental. It has escaped from cultivation and occurs throughout the parks.

Coral ardisia (*Ardisia crenata*), native to Japan and southern Asia and **garland-flower** (*Hedychium coronarium*), native to tropical Asia, were planted in the Hydric Hammock along the nature trail. Another significant patch of coral ardisia is at Sulfur Spring on the Kittridge Tract. Ardisia drops many berries that sprout new plants. Garland-flowers have extensive roots that easily snap off underground when the plants are pulled. New plants sprout from these old roots.

Japanese climbing fern (*Lygodium japonicum*) is native to the Old World. Under the right conditions, it can spread rampantly and overtake native species.

Sickel pod (*Cassia obtusifolia*), **hairy indigo** (*Indigofera hirsuta*), **lantana** (*La* sp.), **rattle box** (*Crotolaria spectabilis*) and **pasture bean** (*Sesbania vesicaria*) occu in Ruderal areas scattered across the parks. Sickle pod is from tropical America and hairy indigo is from Africa.

Cogongrass occurs in several locations. Recent logging activities appeared to have introduced cogongrass to several remote areas.

Chinese tallow (*Sapium sebiterum*) is native to China and Japan and is sought as an ornamental because the leaves turn bright red during the early winter season. It was discovered in 2002 in great quantities on the Skinner parcel of the Lower Wekiva River Preserve State Park.

Tropical Soda Apple (*Solanum viarum*) is native to South America. It is widespread in RSRSR.

Animals

Nine-banded armadillos (*Dasypus novemcinctus*) and **wild hogs** (*Sus scrofa*) occur but are rarely encountered. Feral cats and dogs (*Canis domesticus*) are also found throughout the parks. Cats tend to be more common around use areas and near fencelines that adjoin private residences.

Rhesus monkeys (*Macaca mulatta*), which are native to India, have been seen along Wekiwa Springs Run and there was once a small colony in Wekiwa Springs State Park. They are suspected to be descendants of a colony that used to be housed at DeLeon Springs when it was a zoo.

European starlings (*Sturnus vulgaris*) occur throughout the park in small numbers.

Greenhouse frogs (*Eleutherodactylus planirestris*) are found throughout the parks.

Brown anoles (*Anolis sagrei*) are common in areas adjoining private residences and in the main use area.

Cuban treefrog (*Osteopilus septentrionalis*) is a relatively new exotic found in the park.

Armored catfish (*Pterygoplichthys disjunctivus*) can be found in large numbers in Wekiwa Springs, Witherington Springs, and Sulfur Springs. The fish congregate at the side spring, especially during cold weather, and can take advantage of the low oxygen conditions in the caves. They feed on small crustaceans, carrion, and occasionally algae. Their powerful burrowing habits have weakened the retaining wall around the main spring.

Hoplosternum littorale) is a native of South America but is now
~~it~~ Central and South Florida. It is also called the armored catfish
~~rows~~ of large hard scales that form plate-like armor along its sides
~~m~~ potential predators.

The **Plecostomus,** or Suckerfish, is another native of South America that is now found throughout Central and South Florida although it has not yet been found within the parks. They are sold in pet stores because they eat algae and keep the glass clean. The trouble is they get big and are often released into the wild. They have heavily armored body that protect them from most predators. They grow to about 18 inches in length and use special rasping lips to tear off their food).

Problem Species

Problem species are native species whose habits create specific management problems or concerns. Occasionally, problem species are also a designated species, such as alligators.

Gray squirrels (*Sciurus carolinensis*) and **raccoons** (*Procyon lotor*) are common problem species.

Florida black bears can also cause significant problems.

A Year in The Life of the Parks

January
Listen for the shrill nocturnal mating calls of the bobcat.
Nesting season starts for Florida sandhill cranes, hawks and owls.
Snail kites begin their courtship.
Listen for the male Cardinals territorial singing.
Black crappies start a feeding frenzy.

February
Look for the return of migratory birds – a sure sign that spring is coming.
Bald eagle chicks are learning to fly and getting ready to leave the nests.
It's breeding season for the Sherman's fox squirrel.
The first litter of gray squirrels is born.

March
Annual Real Florida 5K Run and Fun Walk organized by the Wekiwa Wilderness Trust.
RiverFest organized by Friends of the Wekiva River.
Listen for woodpeckers "hammering" on trees in the early morning or late afternoon to attract mates.
Wood storks begin their courtship.
Scrub jays begin to mate and nest build.
Look up to see the magnificent, soaring swallow tailed kite.
Say cheerio to the wintering American Robin leaving to spend summer up north.
Observe the first green needles appearing on the bald cypress.
Great crested flycatchers return to spend summer in the park.
Tree frogs start to lay their eggs.

April
Listen for the nocturnal calls of the Chuck-will's-widow
The time for prescribed controlled burns.
Bobwhite quail are nesting.
The first cream flowers and bracts of the basswood (American Linden) appear.
River otters give birth.
The southern magnolia bursts into bloom.
Saw palmetto white flowers start to turn into fruit.
Watch for pairs of parent sandhill cranes protectively roaming with their newly hatched offspring.
The eastern bluebirds, summer tanagers and the great crested flycatcher are back in the sandhills in full breeding plumage and fully vocalizing their intentions.

May
Adult alligators start their courtship – listen for the males bellowing.
This is the peak of gator mating season.
Look for ospreys fishing to feed their young.

There are usually more bear sightings in May than any other month.
The white flower clusters of the buttonbush appear.
See if you can spot the blue flowers of the passion flower vine and the Gulf Fritillary butterflies that are attracted to them.
Bear grass blooms with clusters of white flowers.
The pendulous yellow flowers of the yellow star anise appear.
Most bats have their young between now and mid-June.
This is the start of the breeding season for most resident and summer song birds.

June

This is the most dangerous month for wildfires.
It is National Get Outdoors Month.
Seminole bats have their young.
Female alligators are nest building.
This is the height of the gopher tortoise nesting season.
Indigo snakes lay their eggs.

July

Scrub morning glory bursts into bloom.
Virginia creeper is at its most rampant.
Gray squirrels have their second litter of the year.
Start of the bear breeding season.
It's time for the Sherman's fox squirrels' second litter.

August

Look for the brilliant yellow flowers of goldenrod.
Alligators hatch from mid-August.
Indigo snakes and gopher tortoises are hatching.

September

Start of the fall hawk migration.
Bald eagles return to nest sites and start courtship.
Look for the yellow flowers of the partridge pea.
The first whip-poor-wills start to arrive to winter in the park.
Look for water-spider orchids.

October

Warbler migration is in full swing.
Gray foxes start to mate.
Look out for migrating Monarch butterflies.

November

Bald eagles start the nesting preparations for a new brood.
The most dangerous month for black bear being killed on the roads.
White tailed deer start rutting.
Cedar waxwings and American robin arrive for the winter.
Look for the spectacular aerial courtship displays of bald eagles.

December

It's a good time to watch wintering waterfowl on the park lakes
Bobcats mate between December and April and this is the most likely time to spot them.
Barred owls are courting.

Recreation in the Parks

The approximately 15 miles of the Wekiva River, the 8.5 miles of Rock Springs Run, and Wekiwa Springs provide the primary recreational attraction for the Wekiva River Basin State Parks. The National Park Service has designated the Wekiva River as a Wild and Scenic River. Recreational activities on these waters should be limited to canoeing, kayaking, fishing and nature study.

The uplands of the three parks are comprised mainly of Mesic Flatwoods, Sandhill and Scrub communities. They support various recreational activities in addition to diverse opportunities for nature observation, interpretive education, and nature photography.

Swimming

Wekiwa Springs is popular fir swimming and sunning. Estimated peak summer use of the main spring areas is between 1,200 and 1,500 people a day. A bulkhead surrounds the springhead pool and a short portion of the spring-run, allowing easy access.

Hiking In and Around the Parks

All three parks have extensive trail systems. Many trails in the three parks were built and are maintained by volunteers. The Florida Trail Association (FTA) developed and designated several trails as Florida Trail loop trails.

Wekiwa Springs State Park

Hiking trails have been established throughout the park.

Rock Springs Run State Reserve

Recreation in this park focus on the trails. There are marked hiking, biking and equestrian trails and an additional 32 miles of multi-use trails on unpaved roads.

Lower Wekiva River Preserve State Park

Western sections of the park have trails for horseback riders and hikers. Hiking trails are accessible from the SR46 entrance. Also there are multi-use unpaved roads.

The West Orange Trail

This is a multi-purpose recreational trail, managed by Orange County, which runs from State Road 50 (the Lake/Orange County line) to Rock Springs Road in Apopka. The asphalt trail serves pedestrians, skaters and bikers.

The Seminole-Wekiva trail

This is a 14 mile multi-use rail-trail, extends from State Road 436 to Markham Road west of Orange Blvd. It connects to the Rinehart Road Crossings Trail via an overpass over I-4. The Seminole-Wekiva to Cross Seminole Connector connection will create a 30-mile continuous paved trail connecting: Altamonte Springs, Longwood, Lake Mary, Winter Springs, Oviedo and the Cady Way Trail and the Orange County Trails System. The existing Seminole-Wekiva Trail includes a portion of the Florida National Scenic Trail in southern LWRPSP.

Trails in the northern section of Lower Wekiva River Preserve SP connect to trails in Seminole State Forest. This connection will be maintained. Lake County plans are to link Seminole County's Seminole-Wekiva with the Sorrento to Seminole County Line Trail.

Canoeing

Wekiwa Springs Run and the Wekiva River are part of the designated State Canoe Trail.

A canoe rental concession is located on the springs-run at WSSP. One-way trips to Katie's Landing with return shuttle service are available.

There are private canoeing and tubing outfitters located along Rock Springs Run and the Wekiva River. Kings Landing is located on Rock Springs Run and has canoes for rent. Weekends are by far the most popular so choose a weekday to avoid the crowds. Wekiva Marina and Wekiwa Springs State Park also have canoe rentals and offer a shuttle service to canoeists, with several designated drop off and pickup points along the Wekiva River.

The Wekiva River/Rock Springs Run Canoe Trail is officially designated as part of Florida's Statewide System of Greenways and Trails. This canoe trail begins at Kings Landing on Rock Springs Run and continues down the run until it meets the Wekiva River. The trail then travels north, although the river is running downstream, on the Wekiva River.

Rock Springs Run is bordered by Rock Springs Run State Preserve on one side and Wekiwa Springs State Park on the other. The trail passes through Lower Wekiva

State Reserve on its way to the St. Johns River. The mixture of swift and placid water offers a frequent change of pace. Traveling through Sand Pine Scrub, Pine Flatwoods, Hammocks and Swamps, paddlers will see a variety of wildlife including limpkins and white ibis. Quiet observers may see some rare and endangered

species such as the Florida black bear, wood stork and sandhill crane. Numerous islands, tributaries and lagoons provide opportunities for side trips and camping.

It can take three to five hours to canoe from King's Landing to Wekiwa Marina, and then another three hours to paddle from Wekiwa Marina to Katie's Landing. Add another two or three hours to go the next six miles of "Scenic and Wild" Wekiva River to its confluence with the St. Johns River.

Birds to look for on or close to the river include great blue heron, great egret, snowy egret, little blue heron, green-heron, tri-colored heron, ibis, limpkin, belted kingfisher, wood duck, moorhen and wood storks.

Overhead you can spot turkey and black vulture, red shouldered and red tailed hawk, osprey, southern bald eagle and swallow-tailed kite. On the banks you may spot white tailed deer, raccoons, black bears, bobcats and opossums – all mammals – and in the water, playful river otter.

The river is also host to a lot of water critters from gators to several species of turtles, frogs and snakes, and many species of fish

Cycling

Off-road bicycling has become an extremely popular outdoor recreation activity.

Horseback Riding

Lower Wekiva River Preserve State Park. A horse camp equipped with a barn, watering trough, and restroom is located near the north entrance.

Wildlife Watching and Birding

The springs, rivers, lakes, swamps and uplands of the Wekiva River Basin State Parks are considered significant wildlife habitat. They are an important refuge for the Florida black bear, bald eagle, swallow-tailed kite,

Florida scrub-jay, large populations of wading birds, and two species of endemic snails. Over 40 listed species are documented. The area's significance for birding is evident by the inclusion of all three parks within the East Section of the Great Florida Birding Trail. Research and wildlife viewing opportunities abound.

Some useful birding hints:

- Get a really good illustrated guide about Florida's birds
- Go out with a more experienced birder or join a club
- Makes notes about birds you cannot identify in the field and look them up when you get home
- Have a good pair of binoculars or spotting telescope on a tripod to provide stability.

Binoculars and telescopes: A good birding binocular is 8x40 – they are compact while providing good magnification and enough light gathering power to be able you to see the image clearly. Larger magnification binoculars and telescopes allow you to see the subject in greater detail but you have to compensate for handshake. The ideal solution is to use a pair of hi-tech image stabilization binoculars such as the 10x35 Bushnell StableView, which eliminate any handshake and give you a ra-zor sharp, stable image every time. Also, choose an optical device that is waterproof otherwise your lens may fog up inside if it is raining or if the humidity is very high.

Water Conservation

As Florida's population increases, so does the need for all Florida's residents to conserve. Water conservation may seem unnecessary in a state surrounded by water, but not all of that water is readily available for drinking or irrigation.

An adult needs 2.5 quarts of water a day to maintain a healthy body, yet the average water usage per person per day in this area is about 160 gallons. Conserve water by being more conscious of all use, watering plants only when necessary and fixing plumbing leaks promptly. Even a small leak can waste 300 or more gallons of water per month. Saving water also saves money and may reduce time spent on home maintenance, due to mold and mildew damage.

Even with conservation, all future water supply needs will not be able to be met from groundwater alone, but the most important way to help supply is by efficient use. Alternative water sources will need to be developed and alternative management strategies will need to be implemented.

Facts to consider:

- More than 90 percent of the water we use comes from groundwater, water drawn from underground aquifers.

- Florida usually receives about 50 inches of rain each year, but only about 13 inches of water seeps into the ground to replenish underground aquifers.

- Using too much groundwater can result in drying out wetlands, lowering lake levels, reducing spring flows and impairing water quality from saltwater intrusion.

- These unacceptable impacts should not be allowed to occur.

Even with conservation, all future water supply needs will not be able to be met from groundwater alone. Alternative water sources will need to be developed and alternative management strategies will need to be implemented.

One of the most important ways to help meet our water supply needs for today and in the future is through conservation, which is the efficient and effective use of water. Conservation will help sustain our groundwater supplies for as long as possible.

Irrigation

Experts agree that most people water too much and is unhealthy for their grass. Irrigate your lawn when it shows signs of stress from lack of water. Look for signs of stressed grass, such as a bluish-gray color, leaf blades folded in half lengthwise and lingering tire tracks or footprints. You may also determine your lawn's water needs by measuring soil moisture. Water during cool, early morning hours. Water evaporation is increased during the day (up to 60 percent) and when it is windy. Over watering encourages diseases.

If you have an automatic sprinkler system, be sure it is equipped with a working rain shutoff device, which overrides the system when enough rain has fallen. It automatically resets the system when the turf requires more water. Florida law requires rain shutoff devices on all automatic sprinkler systems installed since 1991. Check regularly to ensure the device is working properly and that the corresponding switch in the control box is set at "on."

Drip irrigation is the most efficient method of watering for non-turf areas such as bedded plants, trees or shrubs. Drip systems minimize or eliminate evaporation, impede weed growth, and may help prevent grass diseases caused by under-watering or overwatering. If using a hose sprinkler, place the sprinkler in the driest area. Run the sprinkler long enough to apply one-half to three-quarters of an inch of water and then move the sprinkler to another dry area. Place the sprinkler so that a watering overlap occurs. Adjust the hose or sprinkler so it waters just the grass or shrubs, and not paved areas.

Lawn Maintenance

Cut your grass at the highest recommended height for your turf species, or the highest setting on your lawn mower. Mow regularly, cutting no more than one-third of the grass length to encourage grass roots to grow deep and grass blades to hold moisture.

Keep mower blades sharp. Dull blades tear grass, opening it to disease, and cause it to appear tan and ragged. Leave short grass clippings where they fall, reducing the lawn's need for water and fertilizer. Scatter thick patches of clippings so that clippings will not kill the grass underneath.

Additional Tips

- Do not leave sprinklers unattended. Use a kitchen timer as a reminder to turn sprinklers off.
- Water slowly to reduce runoff and to allow deep penetration.
- Observe the watering schedule for your address.
- Dig out water-loving weeds and cultivate soil often.
- Use a rain barrel to collect rainwater. Rainwater is free and is better for your plants because it doesn't contain hard minerals.

- Do not hose down your driveway or sidewalk. Use a broom to clean leaves and other debris from these areas.

- Use a hose shutoff nozzle on your hose that can be adjusted to a fine spray so that water flows only as needed. When finished, turn it off at the spigot (not the nozzle) to avoid leaks. A garden hose without a shutoff nozzle can pour out 530 gallons of water in an hour.

- Avoid purchasing recreational water toys that require a constant stream of water.

- Consider using a commercial car wash that recycles water. If you wash your own car, park on the grass, use a bucket of soapy water and use a hose with a shutoff nozzle.

- Avoid the installation of ornamental water features (such as fountains) unless the water is recycled.

- If you have a swimming pool, consider a new water-saving pool filter and cover your pool or spa to reduce evaporation.

Volunteering

The Wekiva Wilderness Trust (WWT) is a not for profit Citizens Support Organization dedicated to the preservation and restoration of the natural environment and promotion of nature-related activities within the Wekiva Basin. The organization is made up totally of volunteers and is dependent on contributions for financial support. WWT receives no local, state or federal financial support.

Run by volunteers, the Wekiwa Springs Nature Center aims to introduce visitors to the wealth of wildlife within the park's boundary. Enjoy all the park has to offer and help protect it for future generations by supporting the WWT.

Apart from contributions there are several ways that you can help. Volunteers work in the parks and help with trail maintenance, river clean up, nature walks, research projects and bird mist netting programs. They also assist with park events and a host of WWT activities such as the annual Real Florida 5K Run and Walk.

Join the Wekiva Wilderness Trust and help protect some of Central Florida's most important habitats and wildlife refuges.

For more information visit the WWT's Website at **www.wwt-cso.com** or go to the Park's Website at **www.FloridaStateParks.org/Wekiwa Springs** or write to:

Wekiva Wilderness Trust
1800 Wekiwa Circle
Apopka FL 32712

Field Notes-Animals Tracks

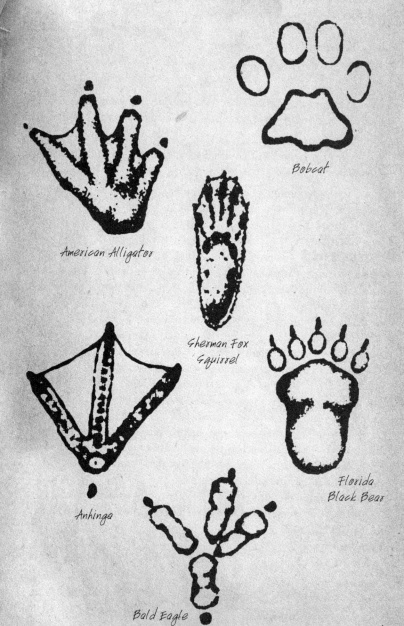

Bobcat

American Alligator

Sherman Fox Squirrel

Anhinga

Florida Black Bear

Bald Eagle

Paul Lammardo

Field Notes-Animals Tracks

Gopher Tortoise

Northern River Otter

Wild Turkey

Grey Fox

Green Treefrog

White Tailed Deer

Paul Lammardo

Appendix 1: PLANTS

Plant	Scientific Name	Habitat Codes
Red maple	*Acer rubrum*	33, 35
Giant leather fern	*Acrostichum danaeifolium*	33
Sticky jointvetch	*Aeschynomene viscidula*	
Red buckeye	*Aesculus pavia*	33, 35
Purple false foxglove	*Agalinis purpurea*	8
Seminole false foxglove	*Agalinis filifolia*	8
Florida hobblebush; Pipestem	*Agarista populifolia*	33, 35
Hammock snakeroot	*Ageratina jucunda*	13,23
Silktree, mimosa *	*Albizia julibrissin*	13
Yellow colicroot	*Aletris lutea*	8
Alligatorweed*	*Alternanthera philoxeroides*	55
Bastard indigobush	*Amorpha fruticosa*	21, 33, 35
Peppervine	*Ampelopsis arborea*	33, 35
Splitbeard bluestem	*Andropogon ternarius*	13
Broomsedge bluestem	*Andropogon virginicus var. virginicus*	8, 13
Green silkyscale	*Anthaenantia villosa*	8,13
Groundnut	*Apios americana*	33
Nodding nixie	*Apteria aphylla*	21
Coral ardisia*	*Ardisia crenata*	35
Jack-in-the-pulpit	*Arisaema triphyllum*	21, 35
Wiregrass	*Aristida beyrichiana*	13,14,15,21
Virginia snakeroot	*Aristolochia serpentaria*	33, 35
Florida indian plantain	*Arnoglossum floridanum*	13
Switchcane	*Arundinaria gigantea*	35
Pinewoods milkweed	*Asclepias humistrata*	13, 8, 81
Whorled milkweed	*Asclepias verticillata*	8,13
Fewflower milkweed	*Asclepias lanceolata*	8, 41, 13
Butterflyweed; Butterfly milkweed	*Asclepias tuberosa*	13
Dwarf pawpaw	*Asimina pygmaea*	13
Netted pawpaw	*Asimina reticulata*	13
Smallflower pawpaw	*Asimina parviflora*	21, 35
Climbing aster	*Aster carolinianus*	33
Whitetop aster; Dixie aster	*Aster tortifolius*	13,14,23
Whitetop aster; Pinebarren aster	*Aster reticulatus*	13
Elliott's aster	*Aster elliottii*	33, 35
Big carpetgrass	*Axonopus furcatus*	8,41,46
Carolina mosquito fern	*Azolla caroliniana*	55

Plant	Scientific Name	Habitat Codes
Groundsel tree; Sea myrtle	*Baccharis halimifolia*	29, 35, 47
Lemon bacopa; Blue waterhyssop	*Bacopa caroliniana*	8, 41
Coastalplain honeycombhead	*Balduina angustifolia*	3, 14
Bamboo *	*Bambusa sp.*	35
Tarflower	*Befaria racemosa*	8, 14, 15
Wax begonia; club begonia*	*Begonia cucullata*	21,32,33,35
Alabama supplejack; Rattan vine	*Berchemia scandens*	21, 33, 35
Florida greeneyes	*Berlandiera subacaulis*	13
Beggarticks; Romerillo	*Bidens alba*	81
Smallfruit beggarticks	*Bidens mitis*	81, 13
Crossvine	*Bignonia capreolata*	33, 35
Toothed midsorus fern; Swamp fern	*Blechnum serrulatum*	8, 41, 46
False nettle, Bog hemp	*Boehmeria cylindrica*	35
Southern grape-fern	*Botrychium biternatum*	23, 35
Paper mulberry*	*Broussonetia papyrifera*	8, 13
American bluehearts	*Buchnera americana*	8,15
Densetuft hairsedge	*Bulbostylis ciliatifolia*	13,14,15
American beautyberry	*Callicarpa americana*	8, 13, 21
Tuberous grasspink	*Calopogon tuberosus*	8, 41
Pale grasspink	*Calopogon pallidus*	41
Manyflowered grasspink	*Calopogon multiflorus*	8, 41
Bandana-of-the-everglades	*Canna flaccida*	41, 33, 53
Chapman's sedge	*Carex chapmannii*	35
Bromelike sedge	*Carex bromoides*	33, 35
Long's sedge	*Carex longii*	32,33,35
Vanillaleaf	*Carphephorus odoratissimus*	13
Coastalplain chaffhead	*Carphephorus corymbosus*	8, 13
American hornbeam; Bluebeech	*Carpinus caroliniana*	33, 35
Pignut hickory	*Carya glabra*	21, 35
Chinquapin	*Castanea pumila*	13,23
Spadeleaf	*Centella asiatica*	32,33,35
Spurred butterfly pea	*Centrosema virginianum*	13, 14, 8
Common buttonbush	*Cephalanthus occidentalis*	33
Florida rosemary; Sand heath	*Ceratiola ericoides*	14
Partridge pea	*Chamaechrista fasciculata*	13,81
Sensitive pea	*Chamaecrista nictitans var. aspera*	8,13,15
Alicia	*Chapmannia floridana*	3, 14, 15
Slender woodoats	*Chasmanthium laxum*	13
Shiny woodoats	*Chasmanthium nitidum*	33, 35

Plant	Scientific Name	Habitat Codes
White fringetree; Old-man's beard	*Chionanthus virginica*	21
Spotted water hemlock	*Cicuta maculata*	32,33
Camphortree *	*Cinnamomum camphora*	8, 21
Nuttall's thistle	*Cirsium nuttallii*	All
Jamaica swamp sawgrass	*Cladium jamaicense*	55
Swamp leather-flower	*Clematis crispa*	21, 35
Bleeding-heart*	*Clerodendrum thomsoniae*	82
Rose glorybower*	*Clerodendrum bungei*	82
Atlantic pigeonwings	*Clitoria mariana*	13
Tread-softly; Finger-rot	*Cnidoscolus stimulosus*	All
Carolina coralbead	*Cocculus carolinus*	21
Wild taro; Dasheen; Coco yam *	*Colocasia esculenta*	55
Whitemouth dayflower	*Commelina erecta*	All
Dayflower	*Commelina diffusa*	All
Blue mistflower	*Conoclinium coelestinum*	35
Spring coralroot	*Corallorhiza wisteriana*	21, 35
Flowering dogwood	*Cornus florida*	21
Swamp dogwood; Stiff dogwood	*Cornus foemina*	33, 35
May haw; May hawthorn	*Crataegus aestivalis*	35
Yellowleaf hawthorn	*Crataegus flava*	21
Slender scratchdaisy	*Croptilon divaricatum*	82
Smooth rattlebox*	*Crotalaria pallida*	13, 81
Showy rattlebox*	*Crotalaria spectabilis*	81
Rabbitbells	*Crotalaria rotundifolia*	All
Woolly croton; Hogwort	*Croton capitatus*	13
Silver croton; Healing croton	*Croton argyranthemus*	13
Rushfoil; Michaux's croton	*Croton michauxii*	8,13,14
Roseling	*Cuthbertia sp.*	13
Florida scrub roseling	*Cuthbertia ornata*	13
Leafless swallowwort	*Cynanchum scoparium*	8,13,14,15,23,35,41
Jointed flatsedge	*Cyperus articulatus*	55
Feay's prairieclover	*Dalea feayi*	14
Summer farewell	*Dalea pinnata var. pinnata*	13
Cowitch vine; Climbing hydrangea	*Decumaria barbara*	21, 33, 5
Western tansymustard	*Descurainia pinnata*	82
Dixie ticktrefoil*	*Desmodium tortuosum*	23, 81
Florida ticktrefoil	*Desmodium floridanum*	13,15,23
Slimleaf ticktrefoil	*Desmodium tenuifolium*	13
Variable witchgrass	*Dichanthelium commutatum*	33, 35

Plant	Scientific Name	Habitat Codes
-----------	*Dichanthelium ensifolium var. breve*	14
Hemlock witchgrass	*Dichanthelium portoricense*	All
Openflower witchgrass	*Dichanthelium laxiflorum*	All
----------	*Dichanthelium ensifolium var. ensifolium*	41,35
Cypress witchgrass	*Dichanthelium dichotomum*	13
Carolina ponysfoot	*Dichondra caroliniensis*	35, 81
Virginia buttonweed	*Diodia virginiana*	26,33,35,41
Poor joe; Rough buttonweed	*Diodia teres*	8,13,15
Air-potato *	*Dioscorea bulbifera*	13,21,81
Common persimmon	*Diospyros virginiana*	8, 13, 21,41,81
Southern wood fern	*Dryopteris ludoviciana*	35
Oblongleaf twinflower	*Dyschoriste oblongifolia*	21,35
Common water-hyacinth*	*Eichhornia crassipes*	55
Tall elephantsfoot	*Elephantopus elatus*	8,21
Carolina elephantsfoot	*Elephantopus carolinianus*	26,35
Carolina scalystem	*Elytraria caroliniensis var. caroliniensis*	8,41
Florida tasselflower*	*Emilia fosbergii*	81
Florida butterfly orchid	*Encyclia tampensis*	21,33,35
Earpod tree*	*Enterolobium contortisiliquum*	81
Green-fly orchid	*Epidendrum conopseum*	35
Golden pothos*	*Epipremnum pinnatum*	35
American burnweed; Fireweed	*Erechtites hieracifolia*	35
Oakleaf fleabane	*Erigeron quercifolius*	13, 81
Prairie fleabane	*Erigeron strigosus*	13,81
Tenangle pipewort	*Eriocaulon decangulare*	8,41
Dogtongue wild buckwheat	*Eriogonum tomentosum*	13,14,15
Fragrant eryngo	*Eryngium aromaticum*	8,13,14,41
Baldwin's eryngo	*Eryngium baldwinii*	8,41,81
Coralbean; Cherokee bean	*Erythrina herbacea*	21
Wild coco	*Eulophia alta*	33,35,41
American strawberrybush	*Euonymus americanus*	33,35
Queen-of-the-meadow; Joepyeweed	*Eupatorium fistulosum*	8, 35, 41
Lateflowering thoroughwort *E.*	*upatorium serotinum*	21,81
White thoroughwort	*Eupatorium album*	13
Dogfennel	*Eupatorium capillifolium*	8,13
Yankeeweed	*Eupatorium compositifolium*	All
Saltmarsh fingergrass	*Eustachys glauca*	8,13
Pinewoods fingergrass	*Eustachys petraea*	13
Green ash; Pumpkin ash	*Fraxinus pennsylvanica*	31

Plant	Scientific Name	Habitat Codes
Carolina ash; Water ash; Pop ash	*Fraxinus carolinianus*	33
Southern umbrellasedge	*Fuirena scirpoidea*	Sand Lake
Elliott's milkpea	*Galactia elliottii*	13,14
Eastern milkpea	*Galactia regularis*	13,23
Soft milkpea	*Galactia mollis*	13, 14
Hairy bedstraw	*Galium pilosum*	All
Oneflower bedstraw	*Galium uniflorum*	13,21,23
Stiff marsh bedstraw	*Galium tinctorium*	35
Garberia	*Garberia heterophylla*	13,14,15
Southern beeblossom	*Gaura angustifolia*	81,13
Blue huckleberry	*Gaylussacia frondosa*	8, 14
Dwarf huckleberry	*Gaylussacia dumosa*	14
Yellow jessamine	*Gelsemium sempervirens*	8,21,35
Sweet everlasting; Rabbit tobacco	*Gnaphalium obtusifolium*	13,81
Loblolly bay	*Gordonia lasianthus*	26,33
Rough hedgehyssop	*Gratiola hispida*	14, 15
Bearded skeletongrass	*Gymnopogon ambiguus*	13
Longhorn false reinorchid	*Habenaria quinqueseta*	35, 41
Toothpetal false reinorchid	*Habenaria floribunda*	35, 41
Waterspider false reinorchid	*Habenaria repens*	35
American witchhazel	*Hammemelis virginiana*	21
English ivy*	*Hedera helix*	81
White gingerlily*	*Hedychium coronarium*	35
Innocence; Roundleaf bluet	*Hedyotis procumbens*	8,21
Southeastern sneezeweed	*Helenium pinnatifidum*	41
Pinebarren frostweed	*Helianthemum corymbosum*	14
Queen-devil	*Hieracium gronovii*	13
Waterthyme*	*Hydrilla verticillata*	55
Manyflower marshpennywort	*Hydrocotyle umbellata*	29,33
Coastalplain spiderlily	*Hymenocallis crassifolia*	55
Pineweeds; Orangegrass	*Hypericum gentianoides*	8
Fourpetal St. John's-wort	*Hypericum tetrapetalum*	13
St. Andrew's-cross	*Hypericum hypericoides*	8
Sandweed; Peelbark St. John's-wort	*Hypericum fasciculatum*	32,41,46,49
Roundpod St. John's-wort	*Hypericum cistifolium*	8
Atlantic St. John's-wort	*Hypericum reductum*	8,14
Yellow stargrass	*Hypoxis sp.*	35
Fringed yellow stargrass	*Hypoxis juncea*	8
Common yellow stargrass	*Hypoxis curtissii*	35

Plant	Scientific Name	Habitat Codes
Clustered bushmint; Musky mint	*Hyptis alata*	35
Scrub holly	*Ilex opaca var. arenicola*	21
Inkberry; Gallberry	*Ilex glabra*	8
Dahoon holly	*Ilex cassine*	26,33,35
Carolina holly; Sand holly	*Ilex ambigua var. ambigua*	21
American Holly	*Ilex opaca var. opaca*	35
Yellow anisetree	*Illicium parviflorum*	33,35,41
Cogongrass *	*Imperata cylindrica*	81,8,14
Carolina indigo	*Indigofera caroliniana*	13,14
Hairy indigo *	*ndigofera hirsuta*	81
Saltmarsh morningglory	*Ipomoea sagittata*	81
Oceanblue morningglory	*Ipomoea indica*	8
Largeroot morningglory* *I*	*pomoea macrorhiza*	13
Man-of-the-earth	*Ipomoea pandurata*	8
Dixie iris; Prairie iris *I*	*ris hexagona*	33,46,47,53,55
Virginia iris	*Iris virginica*	35,41,46,49
Virginia willow	*Itea virginica*	33, 35
Virginia saltmarsh mallow	*Kosteletzkya virginica*	32
Sandspur; Ratany	*Krameria lanceolata*	13, 81
Virginia dwarfdandelion	*Krigia virginica*	21
Carolina redroot	*Lachnanthes caroliniana*	46, 8
Whitehead bogbutton	*Lachnocaulon anceps*	8, 41
Woodland lettuce	*Lactuca floridana*	8,41
Grassleaf lettuce	*Lactuca graminifolia*	13, 81, 8
Lantana; Shrubverbena*	*Lantana camara*	8, 13
Hairy pinweed	*Lechea mucronata*	13,23
Southern cutgrass; Clubhead cutgras	*Leersia hexandra*	46, 55
Duckweed	*Lemna sp.*	55
Lion's-ear; Christmas candlestick*	*Leonotis nepetifolia*	81
Virginia pepperweed	*Lepidium virginicum*	81
Hairy lespedeza	*Lespedeza hirta*	13
Coastal doghobble	*Leucothoe axillaris*	35
Fewflower gayfeather	*Liatris pauciflora*	8,13
Piedmont gayfeather	*Liatris secunda*	13, 14
Shortleaf gayfeather	*Liatris tenuifolia*	8, 13
Gopher apple	*Licania michauxii*	8,13,14
Catesby's lily; Pine lily	*Lilium catesbaei*	8
Florida yellow flax	*Linum floridanum*	8
Sweetgum	*Liquidambar styraciflua*	21,26,33,35

Plant	Scientific Name	Habitat Codes
Tuliptree; Yellow poplar	*Liriodendron tulipifera*	35
Cardinalflower	*Lobelia cardinalis*	55
Glade lobelia	*Lobelia glandulosa*	33,41
Downy lobelia	*Lobelia puberula*	35
Bay lobelia	*Lobelia feayana*	26
Coral honeysuckle	*Lonicera sempervirens*	21,35
Anglestem primrosewillow	*Ludwigia leptocarpa*	47
Creeping primrosewillow	*Ludwigia repens*	33, 47
Skyblue lupine	*Lupinus diffusus*	13,14
Rose-rush	*Lygodesmia aphylla*	13
Japanese climbing fern *	*Lygodium japonicum*	13,35
Fetterbush	*Lyonia lucida*	8
Rusty staggerbush	*Lyonia ferruginea*	14,15
Maleberry	*Lyonia ligustrina*	33,35
Coastalplain staggerbush	*Lyonia fruticosa*	14,15
Marianna maiden fern *	*Macrothelypteris torresiana*	35
Southern magnolia	*Magnolia grandiflora*	21,35
Sweetbay	*Magnolia virginiana*	26,33,35
Southern crabapple	*Malus angustifolia*	23
Angularfruit milkvine	*Matelea gonocarpos*	35
Chinaberrytree*	*Melia azedarach*	21
Creeping cucumber	*Melothria pendula*	21
Noyau vine*	*Merremia dissecta*	8
Browne's savory	*Micromeria brownei*	41
Florida keys hempvine	*Mikania cordifolia*	55
Climbing hempvine	*Mikania scandens*	55
Florida sensitive brier	*Mimosa quadrivalvis var. floridana*	13,14
Sensitive brier	*Mimosa quadrivalvis var. angustata*	13,15
Partridgeberry; Twinberry	*Mitchella repens*	21,35
Lax hornpod	*Mitreola petiolata*	41,47,55
Balsampear*	*Momordica charantia*	8
Spotted beebalm	*Monarda punctata*	21
Indianpipe	*Monotropa uniflora*	14
Red mulberry	*Morus rubra*	21
Southern bayberry; Wax myrtle	*Myrica cerifera*	21,26,29
Tuberous sword fern*	*Nephrolepis cordifolia*	21, 35
Sword fern; Wild Boston fern	*Nephrolepis exaltata*	33, 35
Spatterdock; Yellow pondlily	*Nuphar lutea*	47,55
Big floatingheart	*Nymphoides aquatica*	47

Plant	Scientific Name	Habitat Codes
Swamp tupelo	*Nyssa sylvatica var. biflora*	33,35
Woodsgrass; Basketgrass	*Oplismenus hirtellus*	35
Pricklypear	*Opuntia humifusa*	13,14,15
Goldenclub; Neverwet	*Orontium aquaticum*	47,53,55
Wild olive	*Osmanthus americanus*	21,35
Cinnamon fern	*Osmunda cinnamomea*	33,35
Royal fern	*Osmunda regalis*	33,35
Common yellow woodsorrel	*Oxalis corniculata*	81
Pink woodsorrel*	*Oxalis debilis var. corymbosa*	81
Feay's palafox	*Palafoxia feayi*	13,14,15
Coastalplain palafox	*Palafoxia integrifolia*	13,14,15
Torpedograss*	*Panicum repens*	Sand Lake
Maidencane	*Panicum hemitomon*	29,33
Paronychia *P.*	*aronychia sp.*	13, 14
Virginia creeper; Woodbine	*Parthenocissus quinquefolia*	21,33,35
Egyptian paspalidium	*Paspalidium geminatum*	55
Bull crowngrass	*Paspalum boscianum*	21
Field paspalum	*Paspalum laeve*	8,41,46,81
Vaseygrass *	*Paspalum urvillei*	35
Purple passionflower	*Passiflora incarnata*	8,21
Buckroot	*Pediomelum canescens*	8,13
White arrow arum; Spoonflower	*Peltandra sagittifolia*	41
Green arrow arum	*Peltandra virginica*	33,35
Elephantgrass; Napiergrass*	*Pennisetum purpureum*	32,33,81
Manyflower beardtongue	*Penstemon multiflorus*	13
Red bay	*Persea borbonia var. borbonia*	21
Silk bay, scrub bay	*Persea borbonia var. humilis*	14
Swamp bay	*Persea palustris*	33,35
Savannah panicum	*Phanopyrum gymnocarpon*	33,35
Golden polypody	*Phlebodium aureum*	35,41
Florida false sunflower	*Phoebanthus grandiflora*	13
Oak mistletoe	*Phoradendron leucarpum*	Many
Red chokeberry	*Photinia pyrifolia*	41,53
Turkey tangle fogfruit; Capeweed	*Phyla nodiflora*	23,81
Husk tomato	*Physalis pubescens*	13
American pokeweed	*Phytolacca americana*	All
Wild pennyroyal	*Piloblephis rigida*	8,14,15
Small butterwort	*Pinguicula pumila.*	8,41
Yellow butterwort	*Pinguicula lutea*	8,41

Plant	Scientific Name	Habitat Codes
Blueflower butterwort	*Pinguicula caerulea*	8
Loblolly pine	*Pinus taeda*	35,41
Longleaf pine	*Pinus palustris*	8,14,41
Pond pine	*Pinus serotina*	8,41
Sand pine	*Pinus clausa*	8,13,14,15
Slash pine	*Pinus elliottii*	8,41
Florida needlegrass	*Piptochaetium avenacioides*	13,14
Water-lettuce*	*Pistia stratiotes*	55
Narrowleaf silkgrass	*Pityopsis graminifolia*	13,14,15
Resurrection fern	*Pleopeltis polypodioides var. michauxiana*	21,23
Stinking camphorweed	*Pluchea foetida*	8,41
Sweetscent	*Pluchea odorata*	33
Rosy camphorweed	*Pluchea rosea*	13
Rose pogonia; Snakemouth orchid	*Pogonia ophioglossoides*	41
Showy milkwort	*Polygala grandiflora*	13,21
Coastalplain milkwort	*Polygala setacea*	8
Orange milkwort	*Polygala lutea*	41
Yellow milkwort	*Polygala rugelii*	8,41
King Solomon's seal	*Polygonatum biflorum*	21
Tall jointweed	*Polygonella gracilis*	13,14
Largeflower jointflower	*Polygonella fimbriata var. robusta*	13
Denseflower knotweed	*Polygonum densiflorum*	35
Comb polypody	*Polypodium ptilodon*	23,35
Rustweed; Juniperleaf	*Polypremum procumbens*	46,49
Pickerelweed	*Pontederia cordata*	47
Carolina laurelcherry	*Prunus caroliniana*	21
Black cherry	*Prunus serotina var. serotina*	21
Flatwoods plum; Hog plum	*Prunus umbellata*	21
Chickasaw plum	*Prunus angustifolia*	21,81C
Whisk-fern	*Psilotum nudum*	33,35
Wild coffee	*Psychotria nervosa*	21,35,41
Shortleaf wild coffee	*Psychotria sulzneri*	35
Common hoptree; Wafer ash	*Ptelea trifoliata*	21
Bracken fern	*Pteridium aquilinum*	8,21
Blackroot	*Pterocaulon pycnostachyum*	41
Giant orchid	*Pteroglossaspis ecristata*	13
Carolina desertchicory	*Pyrrhopappus carolinianus*	21
Myrtle oak	*Quercus myrtifolia*	13,14,15
Virginia live oak	*Quercus virginiana*	21,35

Plant	Scientific Name	Habitat Codes
Water oak	*Quercus nigra*	35
Dwarf live oak	*Quercus minima*	14,15
Turkey oak	*Quercus laevis*	13
Scrub oak	*Quercus inopina*	14
Running oak	*Quercus pumila*	14
Small post oak	*Quercus stellata var. margaretta*	13
Bluejack oak	*Quercus incana*	13,14,15
Sand live oak	*Quercus geminata*	13,14,15
Spanish oak; Southern red oak	*Quercus falcata*	21
Chapman's oak	*Quercus chapmanii*	14,15
Laurel oak; Diamond oak	*Quercus laurifolia*	21,35
Needle palm	*Rhapidophyllum hystrix*	35
Fringed meadowbeauty	*Rhexia petiolata*	41
Pale meadowbeauty	*Rhexia mariana*	29,41
Swamp azalea	*Rhododendron viscosum var. serrulatum*	33,41
Winged sumac	*Rhus copallina*	8,21
Rose natalgrass*	*Rhynchelytrum repens*	13
Least snoutbean	*Rhynchosia minima*	13
Michaux's snoutbean	*Rhynchosia michauxii*	13
Doubleform snoutbean	*Rhynchosia difformis*	13
Dollarleaf	*Rhynchosia reniformis*	13
Gray's beaksedge	*Rhynchospora grayii*	13
Sandyfield beaksedge	*Rhynchospora megalocarpa*	13,14
Fragrant beaksedge	*Rhynchospora odorata*	33,35,47
Shortbristle horned beaksedge	*Rhynchospora corniculata*	55
Millet beaksedge	*Rhynchospora miliacea*	33,35
Narrowfruit horned beaksedge	*Rhynchospora inundata*	55
Tropical Mexican clover*	*Richardia brasiliensis*	81
European watercress*	*Rorippa nasturtium-aquaticum*	53
Swamp rose	*Rosa palustris*	33
Sand blackberry	*Rubus cuneifolius*	8
Sawtooth blackberry	*Rubus argutus*	8
Blackeyed susan	*Rudbeckia hirta*	13,15
Carolina wild petunia	*Ruellia caroliniensis*	All
Heartwing dock; Hastateleaf dock	*Rumex hastatulus*	81
Swamp dock	*Rumex verticillatus*	33
Dwarf palmetto; Bluestem palm	*Sabal minor*	21,35
Cabbage palm	*Sabal palmetto*	8,21,33,35
Largeflower rosegentian	*Sabatia grandiflora*	41

Plant	Scientific Name	Habitat Codes
Shortleaf rosegentian	*Sabatia brevifolia*	8,41
Coastal rosegentian	*Sabatia calycina*	35,41
Sugarcane plumegrass	*Saccharum giganteum*	8,32,41
American cupscale	*Sacciolepis striata*	13
Leafless beaked ladiestresses	*Sacoila lanceolata var. lanceolata*	15,23
Broadleaf arrowhead	*Sagittaria latifolia*	33,46
Bulltongue arrowhead	*Sagittaria lancifolia*	33,47
Carolina willow	*Salix caroliniana*	55
Lyreleaf sage	*Salvia lyrata*	8,21
American elder; Elderberry	*Sambucus canadensis*	47
Canadian blacksnakeroot	*Sanicula canadensis*	21,35
Bowstring hemp*	*Sansevieria hyacinthoides*	81
Popcorntree; Chinese tallowtree *	*Sapium sebiferum*	8,13,21,81
Hooded pitcherplant	*Sarracenia minor*	8,41
Sassafras	*Sassafras albidum*	21
Lizard's tail	*Saururus cernuus*	33,55
Florida feathershank	*Schoenocaulon dubium*	13.14
Cuban bulrush*	*Scirpus cubensis*	55
Giant bulrush; California bulrush	*Scirpus californicus*	55
Tall nutgrass; Whip nutrush	*Scleria triglomerata*	8,15,41
Littlehead nutrush	*Scleria oligantha*	33
Fringed nutrush	*Scleria ciliata var. ciliata*	13
Florida scrub skullcap	*Scutellaria arenicola*	14
Helmet skullcap	*Scutellaria integrifolia*	13,14,15
Butterweed	*Senecia glabellus*	8,41,46
Coffeeweed; Sicklepod	*Senna obtusifolia*	81
Saw palmetto	*Serenoa repens*	8,21,35
Yellow bristlegrass; Yellow foxtail	*Setaria parviflora*	32,35,41
Piedmont blacksenna	*Seymeria pectinata*	13,14
Gum bully	*Sideroxylon lanuginosum*	13
Tough bully	*Sideroxylon tenax*	14,15
Starry rosinweed	*Silphium asteriscus*	13
Narrowleaf blueeyed grass	*Sisyrinchium angustifolium*	8,41
Earleaf greenbrier	*Smilax auriculata*	8,21
Saw greenbrier	*Smilax bona-nox*	8,21
Laurel greenbrier	*Smilax laurifolia*	35
Sarsaparilla vine	*Smilax pumila*	21
Jackson vine; Lanceleaf greenbrier	*Smilax smallii*	21,35
Tropical soda apple*	*Solanum viarum*	81

Plant	Scientific Name	Habitat Codes
Chapman's goldenrod	*Solidago odora var. chapmanii*	8
Spiny sowthistle*	*Sonchus asper*	81
Lopsided Indiangrass	*Sorghastrum secundum*	8,13
Spring ladiestresses	*Spiranthes vernalis*	81,8
Pineywoods dropseed	*Sporobolus junceus*	13
Florida hedgenettle; Florida betony	*Stachys floridana*	8
Sweet shaggytuft	*Stenandrium dulce*	8
Queensdelight	*Stillingia sylvatica*	13
Pineland scalypink	*Stipulicida setacea*	13,14
Coastalplain dawnflower	*Stylisma patens*	13,14
Carolina false vervain	*Stylodon carneum*	13
Sidebeak pencilflower	*Stylosanthes biflora*	13
Yellow hatpins	*Syngonanthus flavidulus*	8,41
Bald-cypress	*Taxodium distichum*	26,33,35
Florida hoarypea	*Tephrosia florida*	21
Wood sage; Canadian germander	*Teucrium canadense*	32,35
Widespread maiden fern	*Thelypteris kunthii*	33,35
Hottentot fern; Willdenow's fern	*Thelypteris interrupta*	35
Downy maiden fern	*Thelypteris dentata*	35
Marsh fern	*Thelypteris palustris*	32,35
Carolina basswood	*Tilia americana var. caroliniana*	33,35
Bartram's airplant	*Tillandsia bartramii*	23,35
Ballmoss	*Tillandsia recurvata*	8,14,21
Southern needleleaf	*Tillandsia setacea*	21
Spanish moss	*Tillandsia usneoides*	8,14,21
Eastern poison ivy	*Toxicodendron radicans*	8,21
Poison sumac	*Toxicodendron vernix*	21,35
Bluejacket; Ohio spiderwort	*Tradescantia ohiensis*	13
Forked bluecurls	*Trichostema dichotomum*	8,21
Eastern gamagrass	*Tripsacum dactyloides*	32,33,35,53
Southern cattail	*Typha domingensis*	55
American elm; Florida elm	*Ulmus americana*	35
Caesarweed	*Urena lobata*	8,21
Floating bladderwort	*Utricularia inflata*	46
Zigzag bladderwort	*Utricularia subulata*	41,46
Darrow's blueberry	*Vaccinium darrowii*	13,14
Highbush blueberry	*Vaccinium corymbosum*	8,21
Shiny blueberry	*Vaccinium myrsinites*	8,13,14
Deerberry	*Vaccinium stamineum*	8,13,14

Plant	Scientific Name	Habitat Codes
Tapegrass; American eelgrass	*Vallisneria americana*	55
Common mullein*	*Verbascum thapsis*	81
White crownbeard; frostweed	*Verbesina virginica*	13,14,81
Giant ironweed	*Vernonia gigantea*	21,35
Tall ironweed	*Vernonia angustifolia*	8,21
Water speedwell*	*Veronica anagallis-aquatica*	81
Walter's viburnum	*Viburnum obovatum*	35
Florida vetch	*Vicia floridana*	35,47,55
Common blue violet	*Viola sororia*	23
Early blue violet	*Viola palmata*	8,13
Summer grape	*Vitis aestivalis*	8,21
Calloose grape	*Vitis shuttleworthii*	21
Muscadine	*Vitis rotundifolia*	14,23,35
Shoestring fern	*Vittaria lineata*	33,35
Creeping oxeye*	*Wedelia trilobata*	33,35
Virginia chain fern	*Woodwardia virginica*	33,35
Netted chain fern	*Woodwardia areolata*	33,35
Arrowleaf elephantear*	*Xanthosoma sagittifolium*	33,35
Tallow wood; Hog plum	*Ximenia americana*	35
Coastalplain yelloweyed grass	*Xyris ambigua*	8,41,29
Savannah yelloweyed grass	*Xyris flabelliformis*	8
Spanish bayonet; Aloe yucca*	*Yucca aloifolia*	81
Adam's needle	*Yucca filamentosa*	13,14
Florida arrowroot; Coontie	*Zamia pumila*	21,23
Soldier's orchid; Lawn orchid*	*Zeuxine strateumatica*	81
Crowpoison; Osceola's plume	*Zigadenus densus*	8,41
Annual wild rice; Indian rice	*Zizania aquatica*	55
Viperina	*Zornia bracteata*	8,13,15

* **Non-native Species**

Appendix 2: INVERTEBRATES

Invertebrate	Scientific Name	Habitat Codes
BEETLES		
Eyed click beetle	*Alaus oculatus*	35,41
Scrub beetle	*Gerstaekeria hubbardi*	13
Whirlabout	*Polites vibex*	Throughout
Ox beetle	*Staegus antacus*	8,13
GRASSHOPPERS		
Eastern lubber	*Romalea microptera*	Throughout
Mole cricket	*Scapteriscus vicinus*	Throughout
ANTS		
Ant	*Aphaenogaster carolinensis*	35
Ant	*Aphaenogaster flemingi*	8
Ant	*Aphaenogaster fulva*	35
Ant	*Aphaenogaster lamellidens*	13
Florida harvester ant	*Aphaenogaster treatae*	8,13
Subfamily Formininae	*Brachymyrmex depilis*	8,13,35
Ant	*Brachymyrmex obscurior*	8,13
Florida Carpenter Ant	*Camponotus abdominalis floridanus*	8,13,35
Ant	*Camponotus castaneus*	8,35
Ant	*Camponotus impressus*	35
Ant	*Camponotus nearcticus*	8,13
Carpenter ant	*Camponotus socius*	13
Ant	*Cardiocondyla emeryi**	13
Ant	*Crematogaster ashmeadi*	8,13,35
Ant	*Crematogaster cerasi*	8,13
Ant	*Crematogster minutissima*	35
Ant	*Crytopone gilva*	35
Ant	*Cyphomyrmex septemtrionalis*	8,13,35
Ant	*Discothyrea testacea*	35
Ant	*Dorymyrex bossuta*	13
Ant	*Dorymyrmex bureni*	8,13
Ant	*Eurhopalothrix floridana*	35
Ant	*Forelius pruinosis*	8,13
Ant	*Formica pallidefulva*	8, 13
Ant	*Hypoponera opaciceps*	13,35
Ant	*Hypoponera opacior*	8,13,35

Invertebrate	Scientific Name	Habitat Codes
Cornfiled ant	*Lasius alienus*	35
Ant	*Leptogenys manni*	35
Ant	*Leptothorax pergandei*	8,13
Ant	*Leptothorax texanus*	8,13
Ant	*Myrmecina americana*	35
Subfamily Ecitoninae	*Neivamyrmex opacithoralis*	8,13
Subfamily Dolichoderinae	*Ochetellus glabra*	8
Ant	*Odontomachus brunneus*	35
Ant	*Paratrechina arenivaga*	8, 13
Ant	*Paratrechina bourbonica**	
Ant	*Paratrechina concinna*	8, 35
Ant	*Paratrechina faisonensis*	35
Ant	*Paratrechina longicornis**	
Ant	*Paratrechina wojciki*	8, 13
Ant	*Pheidole dentata*	8,13,35
Ant	*Pheidole dentigula*	8,13,35
Ant	*Pheidole floridana*	8,13,35
Ant	*Pheidole moernes**	8,13,35
Ant	*Pheidole morrisi*	8,13
Florida Harvester ant	*Pogonomyrmex badius*	13
Subfamily Poncrinae	*Proceratium silaceum*	35
Ant	*Pseudomyrex ejectus*	35
Subfamily Pseudimytmecinae	*Pseudomyrmex mexicanus**	13,35
Ant	*Smithistruma angulata*	8
Ant	*Smithistruma laevinasis*	35
Ant	*Smithistruma ornata*	35
Ant	*Smithistruma pulchella*	35
Ant	*Smithistruma talpa*	13.35
Ant	*Solenopsis abdita*	8,13,35
Ant	*Solenopsis carolinesis*	8,13,35
Ant	*Solenopsis geminata*	
Imported fire ant*	*Solenopsis invicta**	8
Ant	*Solenopsis nekersoni*	8,13
Ant	*Solenopsis picta*	35
Ant	*Strumigenys eggersi**	35
Ant	*Strumigenys louisianae*	13,35
Ant	*Strumigenys rogeri**	13,35
Ant	*Trachymyrmex septentrionalis*	8, 13
Ant	*Trichoscapa membranifera**	13
Ant	*Xenomyrmex floridanus*	35

Invertebrate	Scientific Name	Habitat Codes

DAMSELFLIES

Ebony jewelwing .... *Calopteryx maculate* 53, 55

Sparkling jewelwing .... *Calopteryx dimidiate* 53, 55

Fragile forktail .... *Ischnura posita* 53, 55

Variable dancer .... *Argia fumipennis* 53, 55

Duckweed firetail .... *Telebasis byersi* 53, 55

Smoky rubyspot .... *Hetaerina titia* 53, 55

Blue damselfly .... *Enallgma civile* 53,55

DRAGONFLIES

Common green darner .... *Anax junius* 53,55

Regal darner .... *Coryphaeschna ingens* 53,55

Blue dragonlet .... *Erythrodiplax connata minuscula* 53,55

Eastern pondhawk .... *Erythemis simplicicollis* 53, 55

Two-striped forceptail .... *Aphylla williamsoni* 53, 55

Eastern amberwing .... *Perithemis tenera* 53, 55

Black-shouldered spinyleg .... *Dromogomphus spinosus* 53, 55

Prince baskettail .... *Epitheca princeps* 53, 55

Greater hyacinth glider .... *Miathyria marcella* 53, 55

Cypress clubtail .... *Gomphus minutus* 53,55

FLIES

Love bug .... *Plecia nearctica* .... Throughout

Striped horse fly .... *Tabanus lineola* .... Throughout

Crane fly .... *Tipula abdominalis* .... Throughout

Spottedwinged antlion .... *Dendoleon obsoletus* 13,14,15

Coconut mealybug .... *Nipaeciccus nipae* 21

WASPS

Gall wasp .... *Callirhytis cornigera* 13

Velvet ant .... *Dasymutilla occidentalis* 14,15

MOTHS

Luna moth .... *Actias luna* .... Throughout

Polyphemus moth .... *Antheraea polyphemus* .... Throughout

Io moth .... *Automeris io* .... Throughout

Imperial moth .... *Eacles imperialis* .... Throughout

Sphinx moth .... *Enyo lugubris* .... Throughout

Tent caterpillar moth .... *Malacosoma americanum* .... Throughout

Invertebrate	Scientific Name	Habitat Codes
Plume moth	*Oidaematophorus balanotes*	Throughout
Oleander moth	*Syntomeida jucundissima*	Throughout

BUTTERFLIES

White peacock	*Anartia jatrophae guantanamo*	
Least Skipper	*Ancyloxpha numitor*	Throughout
Monk Skipper	*Asbolis capucinus*	Throughout
Great southern white	*Ascia monuste phileta*	Throughout
Hackberry emperor	*Asterocampa celtis alicia*	Throughout
Sachem	*Atalopedes campestris*	Throughout
Delaware skipper	*Atrytone logan*	
Pipevine swallowtail	*Battus philenor philenor*	Throughout
Polydamas swallowtail	*Battus polydamas lucayas*	Throughout
Red-banded hairstreak	*Calycopis cecrops*	Throughout
Southern dogface butterfly	*Colias cesonia*	
Queen butterfly	*Danaus gillippus berenice*	Throughout
Monarch or milkweed butterfly	*Danaus plexippus*	Throughout
Gulf fritillary	*Dione vanilla nigrior*	Throughout
Southern pearly eye	*Enodia portlandia*	Throughout
Silver-spotted skipper	*Epargyreus clarus*	Throughout
Sleepy duskywing	*Erynnis brizo*	
Horace's duskywing	*Erynnis horatius*	
Zarucco duskywing	*Erynnis zarucco*	Throughout
Palmetto skipper	*Euphyes arpa*	Throughout
Dun skipper	*Euphyes vestris*	Throughout
Barred sulphur butterfly	*Eurema daira*	
Barred yellow	*Eurema daira daira*	Throughout
Little yellow butterfly	*Eurema lisa* Throughout	
Sleepy orange	*Eurema nicippe* Throughout	
Zebra swallowtail	*Eurytides marcellus floridensis* Throughout	
Souther hairstreak	*Fixsenia favonius favonius* Throughout	
Sandhill clubtail	*Gomphus cavillaris*	82
Blackwater clubtail	*Gomphus dilatatus*	53,55
Lichen mantis	*Gonatista grisea*	13
Twilight darner	*Gynacantha nervosa*	53,55
Zebra longwing butterfly	*Heliconius charitonius tuckeri*	Throughout
Mayfly	*Heptagenia flavescens*	53,55
Ceraunus blue	*Heriargus ceraunus antbubastus*	Throughout
Carolina satyr	*Hermeuptychia hermes sosybius*	Throughout

Invertebrate	Scientific Name	Habitat Codes
Dotted skipper	*Hesperia atalus*	Throughout
Fiery skipper	*Hylephila phyleus*	Throughout
Cassius blue	*Lepotes cassius theonus*	
Clouded skipper	*Lerema accius*	Throughout
Eufala skipper	*Lerodea eufala*	Throughout
Viceroy	*Limenitis archippus floridensis*	Throughout
Yucca giant-skipper	*Megathymus yuccae*	Throughout
Little wood satyr	*Megisto cymela*	Throughout
Viola's wood satyr	*Megisto viola*	Throughout
Neamathla skipper	*Nastra neamathla*	Throughout
Dainty sulphur	*Nathalis iole*	Throughout
Twin-spot skipper	*Oligoria maculata*	Throughout
Ocola skipper	*Panoquina ocola*	Throughout
Giant swallowtail	*Papilio cresphontes*	Throughout
Eastern tiger swallowtail	*Papilio glaucus australis*	Throughout
Palamedes swallowtail	*Papilio palamedes*	Throughout
American swallowtail	*Papilio polyxenes asterius*	Throughout
Spice-bush swallowtail	*Papilio troilus ilioneus*	Throughout
White M hairstreak	*Parrhasius m-album m-album*	Throughout
Orange-barred sulphur	*Phoebis philea*	Throughout
Cloudless sulfur	*Phoebis sennae eubule*	Throughout
Phaon cresent butterfly	*Phyciodes phaon*	Throughout
Pearl crescent	*Phyciodes tharos tharos*	Throughout
Tawny-edged skipper	*Polites themistocles*	Throughout
Checkered white butterfly	*Pontia protodice*	Throughout
Buckeye butterfly	*Precis coenia*	Throughout
Byssus skipper	*Problema byssus*	Throughout
Tropical checkered-skipper	*Pyrgus oileus*	Throughout
Gray hairstreak	*Strymon melinus melinus*	Throughout
Southern cloudywing	*Thorybes bathyllus*	
Confused cloudywing	*Thorybes confusis*	
Northern cloudywing	*Thorybes pylades*	Throughout
Dorantes longtail	*Urbanus dorantes*	Throughout
Long-tailed skipper	*Urbanus proteus*	Throughout
Red admiral butterfly	*Vanessa atalanta rubria*	Throughout
American lady butterfly	*Vanessa virginiensis*	Throughout
Southern Broken-Dash	*Wallengrenia otho*	Throughout
Zarcco duskywing	*Zerynnis zarucco*	Throughout

Invertebrate	Scientific Name	Habitat Codes

SPIDERS/SCORPIONS

Blue purse-web spider .... *Sphodros abboti*

Arachnid .... *Dermatophagoides* sp. 13

Arachnid .... *Mexecheles hawaiiensis* 13

Arachnid .... *Micrathena gracilis* 13

Arachnid .... *Misumenoides formosipes* 41

Giant vinegaroon .... *Mastigoproctus giganteus* 13

Vinegaroon .... *Idiogaryops paludis* 13

CRAYFISH/MUSSELS/SNAILS/AMPHIPODS/ISOPODS

Orlando cave crayfish .... *Procambarus acherontis* .... Wekiwa Springs Cave

Crayfish .... *Procambarus fallax* 55

Crayfish .... *Procambarus geodytes* 55

Wekiwa hydrobe .... *Aphaostracon monas* .... Wekiwa Springs

Wekiwa siltsnail .... *Cincinnatia wekiwae* .... Wekiwa Springs

Asian clam .... *Corbicula fluminea** 53,55

Mussel .... *Corbicula manilensis* .... RSR, Wekiva River

Mussel .... *Elliptio* sp .... RSR, Wekiva River

Mussel .... *Melanoides turriculus* .... Wekiwa Spgrings

Mussel .... *Planorbella duryi* ssp.* .... Wekiwa Springs

Iridescent liliput mussel .... *Toxoplasma paulus* 53,55

Florida rainbow mussel .... *Villosa amygdala* 53,55

Gastropod .... *Tryonia aequicostata* .... Wekiwa Springs

Gastropod .... *Palaemonetes paludosus* 55

Amphipod .... *Hyalella* sp. .... Wekiwa Springs

Silverfish .... *Lepisma saccharina* 82

Isopod .... *Lirceus* sp. 55

Hobbs cave amphipod .... *Crangonyx hobbsi* .... Wekiwa Springs Cave

Florida cave isopod .... *Caecidotea hobbsi* .... Wekiwa Springs Cave

* Non-native Species

Appendix 3: FISH

Fish	Scientific Name	Habitat Codes
DASYATIDAE		
Sea lamprey	*Petromyzon marinus*	55
Atlantic stingray	*Dasyatis sabina*	33,35
LEPISOSTEIDAE		
Longnose gar	*Lepisosteus osseus*	47,53,55
Florida gar	*Lepisosteus platyrhincus*	47,53,55
AMIIDAE		
Bowfin	*Amia calva*	47,53,55
CYPRINIDAE		
Golden shiner	*Notomigonus chrysoleucas*	53,55
Ironcolor shiner	*Notropis chalybaeus*	53,55
Tailfin shiner	*Notropis maculatus*	53,55
Coastal shiner	*Notropis petersoni*	53,55
Bluenose shiner	*Notropis welaka*	53,55
Pugnose minnow	*Opsopoeodus emiliae*	53,55
Sailfin shiner	*Pteronotropsis hypselopterus*	53,55
Bluenose shiner	*Pteronotropsis welaka*	53,55
CATOSTOMIDAE		
Lake chubsucker	*Erimyzon sucetta*	47
ATHERINOPSIDAE		
Brook silverside	*Labidesthes sicculus*	53,55
ICTALURIDAE		
Snail bullhead	*Ameiurus brunneus*	53,55
Brown bullhead	*Ameiurus nebulosus*	47,53,55
Channel catfish	*Ictalurus punctatus*	53,55
Tadpole madtom	*Noturus gyrinus*	53,55
LORICARIIDAE		
Radiated Ptero*	*Pterygoplichthys multiradiatus*	55,79
Armored catfish*	*Pterygoglichthys disjunctivus*	55,79

Fish	Scientific Name	Habitat Codes

CALLICHTHYIDAE

Brown hopolo* . . . . *Hopolosternum littorale* 55,79

ESOCIDAE

Chain pickerel . . . . *Esox niger* 47,53,55

APHREDODERIDAE

Pirate perch . . . . *Aphredoderus sayanus* .53,55

CYPRINODONTIDAE

Golden topminnow . . . . *Fundulus chrysotus* 53,55

Seminole killifish . . . . *Fundulus seminolis* 53,55

Bluefin killifish . . . . *Lucania goodei* 53,55

Rainwater killifish . . . . *Lucania parva* 53,55

POECILIIDAE

Western mosquitofish . . . . *Gambusia affinis* 47,53,55

Least killifish . . . . *Heterandria formosa* 53,55

Sailfin molly . . . . *Poecilia latipinna* 47,55

CENTRARCHIDAE

Redbreast sunfish . . . . *Lepomis auritus* 47,53,55,81

Warmouth . . . . *Lepomis gulosus* 47,53,55

Bluegill . . . . *Lepomis macrochirus* 47,53,55,81

Dollar sunfish . . . . *Lepomis marginatus* 53,55

Redear sunfish . . . . *Lepomis microlophus* 53,55,81

Spotted sunfish . . . . *Lepomis punctatus* 53,55,81

Largemouth bass . . . . *Micropterus salmoides* 47,53,55,81

Black crappie . . . . *Pomoxis nigromaculatus* 53,55

PERCIDAE

Swamp darter . . . . *Etheostoma fusiforme* .53,55

Blackbanded darter . . . . *Percina nigrofasciata* .53,55

MUGILIDAE

Striped mullet . . . . *Mugil cephalus* 53,55

* **Non-native Species**

Appendix 4: AMPHIBIANS

Amphibians	Scientific Name	Habitat Codes
PLETHODONTIDAE		
Dwarf salamander	*Eurycea quadridigitata*	33,35
Southeastern slimy salamander	*Plethodon grobmani*	33,35
SALAMANDRIDAE		
Striped newt	*Notophthalmus perstriatus*	46,33,35
Peninsula newt	*Notophthalmus viridescens piaropicola*	46,33,35
SIRENIDAE		
Greater siren	*Siren lacertina*	47,55
Lesser siren	*Siren intermdia*	47,55
AMPHIUMIDAE		
Two-toed amphiuma	*Amphiuma means*	33,46,47,53,55
PELOBATIDAE		
Eastern spadefoot	*Scaphiopus holbrookii*	13
BUFONIDAE		
Oak toad	*Bufo quercicus*	8,13,14,15
Southern toad	*Bufo terrestris*	Throughout
LEPTODACTYLIDAE		
Greenhouse frog *	*Eleutherodactylus planirostris*	Throughout
HYLIDAE		
Florida cricket frog	*Acris gryllus dorsalis*	41,35,33,8
Green treefrog	*Hyla cinerea*	Throughout
Pine woods treefrog	*Hyla femoralis*	8,13,15
Barking treefrog	*Hyla gratiosa*	21,14,15
Squirrel treefrog	*Hyla squirella*	Throughout
Cuban treefrog*	*Osteopilus septentrionalis*	Unknown
Southern spring peeper	*Pseudacris crucifer*	41,33,35
Florida chorus frog	*Pseudacris nigrita verrucosa*	33,35
Little grass frog	*Pseudacris ocularis*	8

Amphibians	Scientific Name	Habitat Codes

RANIIDAE

Florida gopher frog . . . . *Rana capito aesopus* 13,81

Bullfrog . . . . *Rana catesbeiana* 47

Bronze frog . . . . *Rana clamitans* 33,35

Pig frog . . . . *Rana grylio* 47

Florida leopard frog . . . . *Rana utricularia* 33,35,47

MICROHYLIDAE

Eastern narrow-mouthed toad . . . . *Gastrophryne carolinensis* 8,13

* **Non-native Species**

Appendix 5: REPTILES

Reptiles	Scientific Name	Habitat Codes
CROCODYLIDAE		
American alligator	*Alligator mississippiensis*	47,53,55
KINOSTERNIDAE		
Striped mud turtle	*Kinosternon bauri*	47
Florida mud turtle	*Kinosternon subrubrum steindachneri*	47,53,55
Loggerhead musk turtle	*Sternotherus minor minor*	47,53,55
Common musk turtle	*Sternotherus odoratus*	47,53,55
TESTUDINIDAE		
Gopher tortoise	*Gopherus polyphemus*	13,14,15
EMYDIDAE		
Peninsula cooter	*Chrysemys floridana peninsularis*	47,53,55
Florida chicken turtle	*Deirochelys reticularia chrysea*	47,53,55
Florida redbelly turtle	*Chrysemys nelsoni*	47,53,55
Florida box turtle	*Terrapene carolina bauri*	21
Red-eared slider*	*Trachemys scripta elegans*	55
CHELYDRIDAE		
Florida snapping turtle	*Chelydra serpentina*	53,55
TRIONYCHIDAE		
Florida softshell	*Apalone ferox*	47,53,55
GEKKONIDAE		
Indo-Pacific gecko*	*Hemidactylus garnotii*	81,82
African house gecko*	*Hemidactylus mabouia*	81,82
POLYCHRIDAE		
Green anole	*Anolis carolinensis carolinensis*	8,21,35
Brown anole *	*Anolis sagrei sagrei*	81,82,21
PHRYNOSOMATIDAE		
Southern fence lizard	*Sceloporus undulatus undulatus*	8,13,14,15

Reptiles	Scientific Name	Habitat Codes

AMPHISBAENIDAE

Florida worm lizard . . . . *Rhineura floridana* 13,14,15

ANGUIDAE

Eastern slender glass lizard . . . . *Ophisaurus attenuatus longicaudus* 21

Eastern glass lizard . . . . *Ophisaurus ventralis* 21

TEIIDAE

Six-lined racerunner . . . . *Cnemidophorus sexlineatus sexlineatus* 13,14,15

SCINIDAE

Peninsula mole skink . . . . *Eumeces egregius onocrepis* 13,14,15

Southeastern five-lined skink . . . . *Eumeces inexpectatus* 8,13,14,15

Broad-headed skink . . . . *Eumeces laticeps* 21,26,35

Sand skink . . . . *Neoseps reynoldsi* 13, 14, 15

Ground skink . . . . *Scincella laterale* 8,21,26,35

COLUBRIDAE

Florida scarlet snake . . . . *Cemophora coccinea coccinea* 8,13,14,15

Southern black racer . . . . *Coluber constrictor priapus* 21,35

Southern ringneck snake . . . . *Diadophis punctatus punctatus* 21,26,35

Eastern indigo snake . . . . *Drymarchon corais couperi* 13,14

Corn snake . . . . *Elaphe guttata guttata* 8,13,14,15,21,35

Yellow rat snake . . . . *Elaphe obsoleta quadrivittata* 8,21,35

Eastern mud snake . . . . *Farancia abacura abacura* 26,47,55

Rainbow snake . . . . *Farancia erytrogramma erytrogramma* 53,55

Eastern hognose snake . . . . *Heterodon platyrhinos* 8,13,14,15

Common kingsnake . . . . *Lampropeltis getula* 35

Eastern kingsnake . . . . *Lampropeltis getula getula* 35

Scarlet kingsnake . . . . *Lampropeltis trianglulum elapsoides* 8

Eastern coachwhip . . . . *Masticophis flagellum flagellum* 13,14,15

Florida water snake . . . . *Nerodia fasciata pictiventris* 47,53,55

Brown water snake . . . . *Nerodia taxispilota* 47,53,55

Rough green snake . . . . *Opheodrys aestivus* 21,35

Florida pine snake . . . . *Pituophis melanoleucus mugitus* 13,14,15

Pine woods snake . . . . *Rhadinaea flavilata* 8

North Florida swamp snake . . . . *Seminatrix pygaea pygaea* 29,33,46/47,49

Short-tailed snake . . . . *Stilosoma extenuatum* 13,14,15

Central Florida crowned snake . . . . *Tantilla relicta neilli* 13,14,15

Reptiles	Scientific Name	Habitat Codes
Peninsula ribbon snake	*Thamnophis sauritus sackeni*	35,47
Eastern garter snake	*Thamnophis sirtalis sirtalis*	35,47

ELAPIDAE

Eastern coral snake	*Micrurus fulvius fulvius*	8,21,35

VIPERIDAE

Florida cottonmouth	*Agkistrodon piscivorus conanti*	47,53,55
Eastern diamondback rattlesnake	*Crotalus adamanteus*	8
Dusky pigmy rattlesnake	*Sistrurus miliarius barbouri*	8,13,14,15

* Non-native Species

Appendix 6: BIRDS

Birds	Scientific Name	Habitat Codes
GREBES		
Pied-billed grebe	*Podilymbus podiceps*	47
Horned grebe	*Podiceps auritus*	47
PELICANS		
American white pelican	*Pelecanus erythrorhynchos*	47
Brown pelican	*Pelecanus occidentalis*	47
CORMORANTS		
Double-crested cormorant	*Phalacrocorax auritus*	47
DARTERS		
Anhinga	*Anhinga anhinga*	47,53,55
BITTERNS & HERONS		
American bittern	*Botaurus lentiginosus*	47
Great blue heron	*Ardea herodias*	47,53,55
Great egret	*Ardea alba*	47,53,55
Snowy egret	*Egretta thula*	47,53,55
Little blue heron	*Egretta caerulea*	47,53
Tricolored heron	*Egretta tricolor*	47,53,55
Cattle egret	*Bubulcus ibis*	8
Green heron	*Butorides striatus*	47,53,55
Black-crowned night-heron	*Nycticorax nycticorax*	47
Yellow-crowned night-heron	*Nyctanassa violaceus*	53,55
STORKS		
Wood stork	*Mycteria americana*	47,53,55
IBISES		
White ibis	*Eudocimus albus*	47,53,55
Glossy ibis	*Plegadis falcinellus*	47,55
SPOONBILLS		
Roseate spoonbill	*Ajaia ajaja*	47,55

Birds	Scientific Name	Habitat Codes

DUCKS & GEESE

Wood duck	*Aix sponsa*	47,53,55
American wigeon	*Anas americana*	47,55
American black duck	*Anas rubripes*	47,55
Mottled duck	*Anas fulvigula*	47
Blue-winged teal	*Anas discors*	47
Northern pintail	*Anas acuta*	47,55
Green-winged teal	*Anas crecca*	47
Redhead	*Aythya americana*	47,55
Ring-necked duck	*Aythya collaris*	47
Hooded merganser	*Lophodytes cucullatus*	47
Common merganser	*Mergus merganser*	47
Red-breasted merganser	*Mergus serrator*	47

VULTURES, HAWKS, KITES, EAGLES

Black vulture	*Coragyps atratus*	8,21
Turkey vulture	*Cathartes aura*	8,21
Osprey	*Pandion haliaetus*	47
Swallow-tailed kite	*Elanoides forficatus*	35,33
Mississippi kite	*Ictinia mississippiensis*	Flyover
Bald eagle	*Haliaeetus leucocephalus*	8
Northern harrier	*Circus cyaneus*	8
Sharp-shinned hawk	*Accipiter striatus*	8,13,21
Cooper's hawk	*Accipiter cooperii*	8,13,21
Red-shouldered hawk	*Buteo lineatus*	8,21,35
Short-tailed hawk	*Buteo brachyurus*	Flyover
Red-tailed hawk	*Buteo jamaicensis*	8,13
American kestrel	*Falco sparverius*	8
Eastern American kestrel	*Falco sparverius sparverius*	8,13
Merlin	*Falco columbarius*	8
Peregrine falcon	*Falco peregrinus*	8

PHEASANTS & ALLIES

Wild turkey	*Meleagris gallopavo*	8,13,21
Northern bobwhite	*Colinus virginianus*	8,13

RAILS

King rail	*Rallus elegans*	47
Virginia rail	*Rallus limicola*	47

Birds	Scientific Name	Habitat Codes
Sora	*Porzana carolina*	47
Purple gallinule	*Porphyrula martinica*	47
Common moorhen	*Gallinula chloropus*	47,55
American coot	*Fulica americana*	47,55

LIMPKIN
Limpkin	*Aramus guarauna*	47,53,55

CRANES
Sandhill crane	*Grus canadensis*	Flyover
Florida sandhill crane	*Grus canadensis pratensis*	8,81

PLOVERS
Semipalmated plover	*Charadrius semipalmatus*	47
Killdeer	*Charadrius vociferus*	8,47,81

STILTS
Black-necked Stilt	*Himantopus mexicanus*	47

SANDPIPERS
Greater yellowlegs	*Tringa melanoleuca*	47
Lesser yellowlegs	*Tringa flavipes*	47
Solitary sandpiper	*Tringa solitaria*	47
Spotted sandpiper	*Actitis macularia*	47,55
Western sandpiper	*Calidris mauri*	47
Least sandpiper	*Calidris minutilla*	47
Short-billed dowitcher	*Limnodromus griseus*	47
Common snipe	*Gallinago gallinago*	8,21
American woodcock	*Scolopax minor*	8,21

GULLS & TERNS
Laughing gull	*Larus atricilla*	Flyover
Bonaparte's gull	*Larus philadelphia*	Flyover
Ring-billed gull	*Larus delawarensis*	Flyover
Herring gull	*Larus argentatus*	Flyover
Caspian tern	*Sterna caspia*	Flyover
Royal tern	*Sterna maxima*	47
Forster's tern	*Sterna forsteri*	47
Least tern	*Sterna antillarum*	47

Birds	Scientific Name	Habitat Codes

DOVES

Rock dove * .... *Columba livia* 8

Eurasian collared-dove * .... *Streptopelia decaocto* 81

Mourning dove .... *Zenaida macroura* 8,13,21

Common ground-dove .... *Columbina passerina* 8,13,21

CUCKOOS

Black-billed cuckoo .... *Coccyzus erythropthalmus* 21

Yellow-billed cuckoo .... *Coccyzus americanus* 21,35

OWLS

Barn owl .... *Tyto alba* 81

Eastern screech-owl .... *Otus asio* 13,21

Great horned owl .... *Bubo virginianus* 8

Barred owl .... *Strix varia* 21,28,35

GOATSUCKERS

Common nighthawk .... *Chordeiles minor* 8,21

Chuck-will's-widow .... *Caprimulgus carolinensis* 8,21

Whip-poor-will .... *Caprimulgus vociferus* 8,21

SWIFTS

Chimney swift .... *Chaetura pelagica* .... Flyover

HUMMINGBIRDS

Ruby-throated hummingbird .... *Archilochus colubris* 8,21,82

KINGFISHERS

Belted kingfisher .... *Ceryle alcyon* 47,53,55

WOODPECKERS

Red-headed woodpecker .... *Melanerpes erythrocephalus* 8,13,15

Red-bellied woodpecker .... *Melanerpes carolinus* 8,21,28,35

Yellow-bellied sapsucker .... *Sphyrapicus varius* 21,35

Downy woodpecker .... *Picoides pubescens* 8,21

Hairy woodpecker .... *Picoides villosus* 8,21

Northern flicker .... *Colaptes auratus* 8,13

Pileated woodpecker .... *Dryocopus pileatus* 8,21,33,35

Birds	Scientific Name	Habitat Codes

TYRANT FLYCATCHERS

Eastern wood-pewee . . . . *Contopus virens* 21
Yellow-bellied flycatcher . . . . *Empidonax flaviventris* 21
Acadian flycatcher . . . . *Empidonax virescens* 21
Alder flycatcher . . . . *Empidonax alnorum* 8
Least flycatcher . . . . *Empidonax minimus* 21
Eastern phoebe . . . . *Sayornis phoebe* 21,35
Great crested flycatcher . . . . *Myiarchus crinitus* 8,21
Eastern kingbird . . . . *Tyrannus tyrannus* 8,21

SHRIKES

Loggerhead shrike . . . . *Lanius ludovicianus* 13

VIREOS

White-eyed vireo . . . . *Vireo griseus* 21,33,35
Yellow-throated vireo . . . . *Vireo flavifrons* 21,35
Blue-headed vireo . . . . *Vireo solitarius* 21
Philadelphia vireo . . . . *Vireo philadelphicus* 21
Red-eyed vireo . . . . *Vireo olivaceus* 21,35

JAYS & CROWS

Blue jay . . . . *Cyanocitta cristata* 8,21,82
Florida scrub-jay . . . . *Aphelocoma coerulescens* 15
American crow . . . . *Corvus brachyrhynchos* 8,21
Fish crow . . . . *Corvus ossifragus* 8,21

SWALLOWS

Purple martin . . . . *Progne subis* . . . . Flyover
Tree swallow . . . . *Tachycineta bicolor* . . . . Flyover
Northern rough-winged swallow . . . . . . *Stelgidopteryx serripennis* . . . . Flyover
Barn swallow . . . . *Hirundo rustica* . . . . Flyover

TITMICE

Carolina chickadee . . . . *Parus carolinensis* 8,21
Tufted titmouse . . . . *Parus bicolor* 8,21

NUTHATCHES

Red-breasted nuthatch . . . . *Sitta canadensis* 8,21
White-breasted nuthatch . . . . *Sitta carolinensis* 8,21
Brown-headed nuthatch . . . . *Sitta pusilla* 8,21

Birds	Scientific Name	Habitat Codes
WRENS		
Carolina wren	*Thryothorus ludovicianus*	21,35
House wren	*Troglodytes aedon*	21
Sedge wren	*Cistothorus platensis*	47,55
Marsh wren	*Cistothorus palustris*	47,55
KINGLETS		
Golden-crowned kinglet	*Regulus satrapa*	21,28,35
Ruby-crowned kinglet	*Regulus calendula*	21,28,35
GNATCATCHERS		
Blue-gray gnatcatcher	*Polioptila caerulea*	8,13,21,28,35
THRUSHES		
Eastern bluebird	*Sialia sialis*	8
Veery	*Catharus fuscescens*	21
Gray-cheeked thrush	*Catharus minimus*	21
Swainson's thrush	*Catharus ustulatus*	21
Bicknel's thrush	*Catharus bicknelli*	21
Hermit thrush	*Catharus guttatus*	21
Wood thrush	*Hylocichla mustelina*	21
American robin	*Turdus migratorius*	21,28,35
MIMIC THRUSHES		
Gray catbird	*Dumetella carolinensis*	21,35
Northern mockingbird	*Mimus polyglottos*	8,21,82
Brown thrasher	*Toxostoma rufum*	8,21
STARLINGS		
European starling *	*Sturnus vulgaris*	8,21
PIPITS		
American pipit	*Anthus rubescens*	21
WAXWINGS		
Cedar waxwing	*Bombycilla cedrorum*	21,28,35
WOOD WARBLERS		
Blue-winged warbler	*Vermivora pinus*	35

Birds	Scientific Name	Habitat Codes
Golden-winged warbler	*Vermivora chrysoptera*	21
Tennessee warbler	*Vermivora peregrina*	21
Orange-crowned warbler	*Vermivora celata*	21,35
Nashville warbler	*Vermivora ruficapilla*	21
Northern parula	*Parula americana*	13,21
Yellow warbler	*Dendroica petechia*	13,21
Chestnut-sided warbler	*Dendroica pensylvanica*	21,35
Magnolia warbler	*Dendroica magnolia*	21,35
Cape May warbler	*Dendroica tigrina*	21,35
Black-throated blue warbler	*Dendroica caerulescens*	21,35
Yellow-rumped warbler	*Dendroica coronata*	8,21
Black-throated green warbler	*Dendroica virens*	21
Blackburnian warbler	*Dendroica fusca*	21,35
Yellow-throated warbler	*Dendroica dominica*	21,35
Pine warbler	*Dendroica pinus*	8,13,21
Prairie warbler	*Dendroica discolor*	8
Palm warbler	*Dendroica palmarum*	21
Bay-breasted warbler	*Dendroica castanea*	13
Blackpoll warbler	*Dendroica striata*	21
Cerulean warbler	*Dendroica cerulea*	21
Black-and-white warbler	*Mniotilta varia*	21,35
American redstart	*Setophaga ruticilla*	21,35
Prothonotary warbler	*Protonotaria citrea*	33
Worm-eating warbler	*Helmitheros vermivorus*	21
Swainson's warbler	*Limnothlypis swainsonii*	21
Ovenbird	*Seiurus aurocapillus*	21,35
Northern waterthrush	*Seiurus noveboracensis*	21
Louisiana waterthrush	*Seiurus motacilla*	21
Kentucky warbler	*Oporornis formosus*	8
Connecticut warbler	*Oporornis agilis*	21
Common yellowthroat	*Geothlypis trichas*	21,35
Hooded warbler	*Wilsonia citrina*	21
Canada warbler	*Wilsonia canadensis*	21
Yellow-breasted chat	*Icteria virens*	8

TANAGERS

Summer tanager	*Piranga rubra*	21
Scarlet tanager	*Piranga olivacea*	21

Birds	Scientific Name	Habitat Codes

CARDINALS

Northern cardinal . . . . *Cardinalis cardinalis* 8,13,21

GROSBEAKS

Rose-breasted grosbeak . . . . *Pheucticus ludovicianus* 21

Blue grosbeak . . . . *Guiraca caerulea* 21

Indigo bunting . . . . *Passerina cyanea* 21

Painted bunting . . . . *Passerina ciris* 21

SPARROWS AND ALLIES

Eastern towhee . . . . *Pipilo erythrophthalmus* 8,13,14,15

Bachman's sparrow . . . . *Aimophila aestivalis* 14

Chipping sparrow . . . . *Spizella passerina* 21

Field sparrow . . . . *Spizella pusilla* 13

Vesper sparrow . . . . *Pooecetes gramineus* 13

Savannah sparrow . . . . *Passerculus sandwichensis* 21

Grasshopper sparrow . . . . *Ammodramus savannarum* 13

Henslow's sparrow . . . . *Ammodramus henslowii* 8

LeConte's sparrow . . . . *Ammodramus leconteii* 8

Saltmarsh sharp-tailed sparrow . . . . *Ammodramus caudacutus* 47

Fox sparrow . . . . *Passerella iliaca* 13

Song sparrow . . . . *Melospiza melodia* 21

Swamp sparrow . . . . *Melospiza georgiana* 47

White-throated sparrow . . . . *Zonotrichia albicollis* 21

White-crowned sparrow . . . . *Zonotrichia leucophrys* 81

ICTERIDS

Bobolink . . . . *Dolichonyx oryzivorus* 47

Red-winged blackbird . . . . *Agelaius phoeniceus* 47

Eastern meadowlark . . . . *Sturnella magna* 8

Yellow-headed blackbird . . . . *Xanthocephalus xanthocephalus* 47

Rusty blackbird . . . . *Euphagus carolinus* 21

Common grackle . . . . *Quiscalus quiscula* 21

Boat-tailed grackle . . . . *Quiscalus major* 47,55

Brown-headed cowbird . . . . *Molothrus ater* 13

Orchard oriole . . . . *Icterus spurius* 13

Baltimore oriole . . . . *Icterus galbula* 21

Birds	Scientific Name	Habitat Codes

FINCHES

Purple finch .... *Carpodacus purpureus* 21

American goldfinch .... *Carduelis tristis* 21

OLD WORLD SPARROWS

House sparrow * .... *Passer domesticus* 81

* **Non-native Species**

Appendix 7: MAMMALS

Mammals	Scientific Name	Habitat Codes
DIDELPHIDAE		
Virginia opossum	*Didelphis virginiana*	21,26,35
SORICIDAE		
Least shrew	*Cryptotis parva*	8
Northern short-tailed shrew	*Blarina brevicauda*	30
TALPIDAE		
Eastern mole	*Scalopus aquaticus*	21
VESPERTILIONIDAE		
Eastern pipistrelle	*Pipistrellus subflavus*	Throughout
DASYPODIDAE		
Nine-banded armadillo *	*Dasypus novemcinctus*	21
LEPORIDAE		
Eastern cottontail	*Sylvilagus floridanus*	8,13,14
Marsh rabbit	*Sylvilagus palustris*	35
SCIURIDAE		
Gray squirrel	*Sciurus carolinensis*	21,82
Sherman's fox squirrel	*Sciurus niger shermani*	13
Southern flying squirrel	*Glaucomys volans*	13,21
GEOMYIDAE		
Southeastern pocket gopher	*Geomys pinetis*	13
CRICETIDAE		
Eastern harvest mouse	*Reithrodontomys humulis*	14,15,81/82
Cotton mouse	*Peromyscus gossypinus*	8,13
Florida mouse	*Podomys floridanus*	15
Golden mouse	*Ochrotomys nuttalli*	8
Eastern woodrat	*Neotoma floridana*	35
Marsh rice rat	*Oryzomys palustris*	47
Hispid cotton rat	*Sigmodon hispidus*	8

Mammals	Scientific Name	Habitat Codes

MURIDAE

Black rat * .... *Rattus rattus* 82

CANIDAE

Red fox * .... *Vulpes vulpes* 13,21

Gray fox .... *Urocyon cinereoargenteus* 8,13,21,35

Coyote* .... *Canis latrans* 8,13,26,28,35

URSIDAE

Florida black bear .... *Ursus americanus* 8,13,26,28,35

PROCYONIDAE

Raccoon .... *Procyon lotor* 8,13,21,35,82

MUSTELIDAE

River otter .... *Lutra canadensis* 47,53,55

Striped skunk .... *Mephitis mephitis* 21

FELIDAE

Bobcat .... *Felis rufus* 8,35

SUIDAE

Wild pig * .... *Sus scrofa* 33,35

CERVIDAE

White-tailed deer .... *Odocoileus virginianus* 8,13,21

* **Non-native Species**

Appendix 8: Habitat Codes

Terrestrial
1. Beach Dune
2. Bluff
3. Coastal Berm
4. Coastal Rock Barren
5. Coastal Strand
6. Dry Prairie
7. Maritime Hammock
8. Mesic Flatwoods
9. Coastal Grasslands
10. Pine Rockland
11. Prairie Hammock
12. Rockland Hammock
13. Sandhill
14. Scrub
15. Scrubby Flatwoods
16. Shell Mound
17. Sinkhole
18. Slope Forest
19. Upland Glade
20. Upland Hardwood Forest
21. Upland Mixed Forest
22. Upland Pine Forest
23. Xeric Hammock

Palustrine
24. Basin Marsh
25. Basin Swamp
26. Baygall
27. Bog
28. Bottomland Forest
29. Depression Marsh
30. Dome
31. Floodplain Forest
32. Floodplain Marsh
33. Floodplain Swamp
34. Freshwater Tidal Swamp

35. Hydric Hammock
36. Marl Prairie
37. Seepage Slope
38. Slough
39. Strand Swamp
40. Swale
41. Wet Flatwoods
42. Wet Prairie

Lacustrine
43. Clastic Upland Lake
44. Coastal Dune Lake
45. Coastal Rockland Lake
46. Flatwood/Prairie Lake
47. Marsh Lake
48. River Floodplain Lake
49. Sandhill Upland Lake
50. Sinkhole Lake
51. Swamp Lake

Riverine
52. Alluvial Stream
53. Blackwater Stream
54. Seepage Stream
55. Spring-Run Stream

Estuarine
56. Estuarine Composite Substrate
57. Estuarine Consolidate-Substrate
58. Estuarine Coral Reef
59. Estuarine Grass Bed
60. Estuarine Mollusk Reef
61. Estuarine Octocoral Bed
62. Estuarine Sponge Bed
63. Estuarine Tidal Marsh

64. Estuarine Tidal Swamp
65. Estuarine Unconsolidated Substrate
66. Estuarine Worm Reef

Marine
67. Marine Algal Bed
68. Marine Composite Substrate
69. Marine Consolidated Substrate
70. Marine Coral Reef
71. Marine Grass Bed
72. Marine Mollusk Reef
73. Marine Octocoral Bed
74. Marine Sponge Bed
75. Marine Tidal Marsh
76. Marine Tidal Swamp
77. Marine Unconsolidated Substrate
78. Marine Worm Reef

Subterranean
79. Aquatic Cave
80. Terrestrial Cave

Miscellaneous
81. Ruderal
82. Developed
MTC Many Types Of Communities
OF Overflying

Appendix 9. Designated Species

PLANTS

Cinnamon fern . . . . *Osmunda cinnamomea*
Royal fern . . . . *Osmunda regalis*
Comb polypody . . . . *Polypodium ptilodon*
Florida arrowroot; Coontie . . . . *Zamia pumila* CE
Needle palm . . . . *Rhapidophyllum hystrix*
Catesby's lily; Pine lily . . . . *Lilium catesbaei*
Manyflowered grasspink . . . . *Calopogon multiflorus*
Florida butterfly orchid . . . . *Encyclia tampensis*
Green-fly orchid . . . . *Epidendrum conopseum*
Rose pogonia; Snakemouth orchid . . . . . *Pogonia ophioglossoides*
Giant orchid . . . . *Pteroglossaspis ecristata*
Yellow anisetree . . . . *Illicium parviflorum*
Hooded pitcherplant . . . . *Sarracenia minor*
Angularfruit milkvine . . . . *Matelea gonocarpos*
Blueflower butterwort . . . . *Pinguicula caerulea*
Yellow butterwort . . . . *Pinguicula lutea*
Cardinalflower . . . . *Lobelia cardinalis*
Garberia . . . . *Garberia heterophylla*
Chapman's sedge . . . . *Carex chapmannii*

INVERTEBRATES

Wekiwa hydrobe . . . . *Aphaostracon monas*
Wekiwa siltsnail . . . . *Cincinnatia wekiwae*
Blue purse-web spider . . . . *Sphodros abboti*
Orlando cave crayfish . . . . *Procambarus acherontis*
Hobbs cave amphipod . . . . *Crangonyx hobbsi*
Florida cave isopod . . . . *Caecidotea hobbsi*

FISH

Bluenose shiner . . . . *Pteronotropsis welaka*
Snail bullhead . . . . *Ameiurus brunneus*

AMPHIBIANS

Florida gopher frog . . . . *Rana capito aesopus*
Striped newt . . . . *Notophthalmus perstriatus*

REPTILES

American alligator . . . . *Alligator mississippiensis*
Eastern diamondback rattlesnake . . . . *Crotalus adamanteus*
Eastern indigo snake . . . . *Drymarchon corais couperi*

Gopher tortoise. . . . . *Gopherus polyphemus*
Sand skink. . . . . *Neoseps reynoldsi*
Florida pine snake. . . . . *Pituophis melanoleucus mugitus*
Short-tailed snake . . . . *Stilosoma extenuatum*

BIRDS

Brown pelican . . . . *Pelecanus occidentalis*
Snowy egret. . . . . *Egretta thula*
Great egret . . . . *Ardea alba*
Little blue heron . . . . *Egretta caerulea*
Tricolored heron . . . . *Egretta tricolor*
Black-crowned night-heron. . . . . *Nycticorax nycticorax*
Yellow-crowned night-heron . . . . *Nyctanassa violaceus*
White ibis . . . . *Eudocimus albus*
Glossy ibis. . . . . *Plegadis falcinellus*
Roseate spoonbill . . . . *Ajaia ajaja*
Wood stork . . . . *Mycteria americana*
Osprey . . . . *Pandion haliaetus*
Swallow-tailed kite . . . . *Elanoides forficatus*
Bald eagle . . . . *Haliaeetus leucocephalus*
Cooper's hawk. *Accipiter cooperii*
Short-tailed hawk . . . . *Buteo brachyurus*
Eastern american kestrel . . . . *Falco sparverius sparverius*
Merlin. . . . . *Falco columbarius*
Peregrine falcon. . . . . *Falco peregrinus*
Limpkin . . . . *Aramus guarauna*
Florida sandhill crane . . . . *Grus canadensis pratensis*
Caspian tern . . . . *Sterna caspia*
Royal tern . . . . *Sterna maxima*
Least tern . . . . *Sterna antillarum*
Hairy woodpecker. . . . . *Picoides villosus*
Florida scrub-jay . . . . *Aphelocoma coerulescens*
White-breasted nuthatch. . . . . *Sitta carolinensis*
American redstart . . . . *Setophaga ruticilla*
Florida prairie warbler. . . . . *Helmitheros vermivorus*
Worm-eating warbler . . . . *Helmitheros vermivorus*
Louisiana Waterthrush . . . . *Seiurus motacilla*
Painted bunting. . . . . *Passerina ciris*
Bachman's sparrow . . . . *Aimophila aestivalis*

MAMMALS

Florida black bear . . . . *Ursus americanus*
Sherman's fox squirrel . . . . *Sciurus niger shermani*
Florida mouse . . . . *Podomys floridanus*

Further Information

Blackman, W. F. 1973. *History of Orange County, Florida*. Mickler House Publishers: Chuluota, FL. 226pp.

Brooks, H. K. 1981b. *Geologic Map of Florida*. Florida Cooperative Extension Service, Institute of Food Agricultural Sciences. University of Florida: Gainesville, FL.

Coumes, S., J. Radz, and T. Ross. 1997. *Wekiva Ferry Site Survey, An Archaeological and Historical Study, Lake County, Florida*. Florida Department of Environmental Protection: Tallahassee, FL.

Eason, T. H. 2003. *Conservation strategy for the black bear in Florida: Final Report*. Dr. Florida Fish and Wildlife Conservation Commission: Tallahassee, FL. 46pp.

Florida Natural Areas Inventory. 1990. *Guide to the natural communities of Florida*. Florida Natural Areas Inventory and Florida Department of Natural Resources: Tallahassee, FL. 111pp.

Gingerich, Jerry Lee, Florida's Fabulous Mammals, World Publication 1994, 129pp.

Hipes, D., D. R. Jackson, K. NeSmith, D. Printiss, and K. Brandt. 2001. *Field guide to the rare animals of Florida*. Florida Natural Areas Inventory: Tallahassee, FL.

Milanich, J. T. and C. H. Fairbanks. 1980. *Florida Archaeology*. Academic Press, Inc.: New York, NY. 290pp.

Milanich, J. T. 1994. *Archaeology of Precolumbian Florida*. University of Florida: Gainesville, FL. 476pp.

Milanich, J. T. 1995. *Florida Indians and the Invasion from Europe*. University of Florida: Gainesville, FL. 290pp.

Rosenau, J. C., G. L. Faulkner, C. H. Hendry, Jr., and R. W. Hull. 1977. *Springs of Florida*. Florida Department of Natural Resources Geological Bulletin No. 31 (revised): Florida Department of Natural Resources: Tallahassee, FL. 461pp.

Seibert, S. M., S. Glenn, K. J. Bradford, R. R. Bradick, F. Brummer, V. Garfein, K. Green, III, C. Hanson, P. T. Harden, A. E. Keen, C. S. Lee, W. McKinnon, D. McLain, M. F. Melchiori, M. Snyder, and A. E. Vanek. 2003. *Wekiva Basin Area Task Force Final Report: Recomendations for planning and locating the Wekiva Parkway while preserving the Wekiva River Basin ecosystem*. Submitted to Governor Jeb Bush.

Seminole County Planning and Development. 2002. *Vision 2020 Comprehensive Plan, Future Land Use Series – Future Land Use Map*. Seminole County: Sanford, FL.

Small, P. E. 1997. Wekiva River Basin Florida scrub-jay (*Aphelocoma coeruelscens*) population. M.S. Thesis. University of Central Florida: Orlando, FL.

Tebeau, C. W. 1971. *A History of Florida*. University of Miami: Coral Gables, FL. 527pp.

Wood, D. A. 1991. *Official lists of endangered and potentially endangered fauna and flora in Florida*. FloridaGame and Freshwater Fish Commission: Tallahassee, FL. Unpublished report. 23pp.

Wunderlin, R. P. 2003. *Guide to the vascular plants of Florida*. University of Florida: Gainesville, FL. 472pp.

Plants	Mesic Flatwoods	Sandhill	Scrub	Scrub by Flatwoods	Upland Mixed Forest	Xeric Hammock	Baygall	Depression Marshes	Dome swamp	Floodplain marsh	Floodplain swamp	Hydric hammock	Wet flatwoods	Marsh lake	Sandhill upland lake	Blackwater stream	Spring-run streams	Aquatic Cave	Sinkholes
Longleaf pine	Y	Y		Y									Y						
Loblolly pine	Y	Y		Y								Y	Y						
Pond pine					Y								Y						
Wild pine									Y										
Slash pine	Y			Y					Y				Y						
Wiregrass	Y																		
Ash									Y	Y	Y								
Sawgrass														Y	Y				
White alder											Y				Y				
Runner oak	Y																		
Pond cypress									Y										
Bald cypress											Y								
Tupelo																			Y
Ogeechee tupelo											Y								
Water tupelo											Y								
Water hickory											Y								

	Florida Elm	Gallberry	Cabbage palm	Saw palmetto	Bluestem palmetto	Needle palm	Buttonbrush	Scrub hickory	St. Johns-wort	Sweetbay	Swamp bay	Loblolly bay	Swamp dogwood	Swamp tupelo	Swamp titi	Large gallberry	Dwarf huckleberry
Sinkholes																	
Aquatic Cave																	
Spring-run streams																	
Blackwater stream																	
Sandhill upland lake										Y							
Marsh lake						Y				Y							
Wet flatwoods		Y		Y							Y					Y	
Hydric hammock			Y	Y	Y	Y					Y	Y					
Floodplain swamp	Y									Y			Y	Y			
Floodplain marsh						Y											
Dome swamp							Y			Y	Y	Y	Y	Y	Y		
Depression Marshes						Y	Y		Y								
Baygall										Y	Y	Y			Y	Y	
Xeric Hammock				Y													
Upland Mixed Forest		Y															
Scrub by Flatwoods				Y													Y
Scrub				Y				Y									
Sandhill																	
Mesic Flatwoods		Y		Y					Y								Y

Guide to the Wekiva River Basin State Parks 153

	Mesic Flatwoods	Sandhill	Scrub	Scrub by Flatwoods	Upland Mixed Forest	Xeric Hammock	Baygall	Depression Marshes	Dome swamp	Floodplain marsh	Floodplain swamp	Hydric hammock	Wet flatwoods	Marsh lake	Sandhill upland lake	Blackwater stream	Spring-run streams	Aquatic Cave	Sinkholes
Fetterbrush	Y																		
Southern magnolia					Y	Y						Y		Y					Y
Wax myrtle		Y					Y	Y	Y		Y	Y	Y						Y
Dwarf wax myrtle	Y																		
Odorless wax myrtle				Y		Y	Y												
Stagger bush	Y			Y															
Blueberry	Y																		
Dwarf blueberry				Y															
Dog-hobble							Y												
Gopher apple	Y			Y			Y				Y								
Hurrah-bush							Y												
Tarflower	Y																		
Bog buttons	Y																		
Blackroot	Y																		
False foxglove	Y																		
White-topped aster	Y													Y					
Yellow-eyed grass	Y													Y	Y				

Habitat	Cutthroat grass	Turkey Oak	Post Oak	Bluejack oak	Sand live oak	Blackjack oak	Diamond leaf oak	Live oak	Sandpost oak	Water oak	Scrub oak	Laurel oak	Swamp chestnut oak	Chapman's oak	Cypress	American hornbeam	Sparkleberry
Sinkholes							Y	Y		Y							Y
Aquatic Cave																	
Spring-run streams																	
Blackwater stream																	
Sandhill upland lake																	
Marsh lake																	
Wet flatwoods																	
Hydric hammock							Y			Y		Y			Y		
Floodplain swamp																	
Floodplain marsh																	
Dome swamp																	
Depression Marshes																	
Baygall															Y		
Xeric Hammock		Y			Y	Y		Y	Y		Y			Y			Y
Upland Mixed Forest								Y		Y							
Scrub by Flatwoods					Y						Y			Y			
Scrub					Y						Y			Y			
Sandhill		Y	Y	Y					Y								Y
Mesic Flatwoods	Y																

	Mesic Flatwoods	Sandhill	Scrub	Scrub by Flatwoods	Upland Mixed Forest	Xeric Hammock	Baygall	Depression Marshes	Dome swamp	Floodplain marsh	Floodplain swamp	Hydric hammock	Wet Flatwoods	Marsh lake	Sandhill upland lake	Blackwater stream	Spring-run streams	Aquatic Cave	Sinkholes
White alder						Y													
Myrtle oak			Y	Y															
Persimmon		Y			Y	Y													
Fetterbrush						Y			Y										
Winged sumac		Y																	
Pinewoods dropseed		Y																	
Indian grass		Y																	
Wild buckwheat		Y																	
Queen's Delight		Y																	
Yellow foxglove		Y																	
Bracken fern		Y																	
Royal fern									Y	Y		Y							
Chain fern														Y					
Leather fern										Y									
Marsh fern										Y									
Water lily															Y				
Fragrant water lily															Y				

Habitat	Water shield	Runner Oak	Goat's rue	Sand cordgrass	Dotted smartweed	Partridge pea	Dollarweeds	Swamp primrose	Water primrose	Tape grass	Giant cut grass	Floating heart	Creeping beggarwood	Golden club	Smartweed	Bluestem	Pitcher plant
Sinkholes																	
Aquatic Cave																	
Spring-run streams										Y	Y						
Blackwater stream														Y	Y		
Sandhill upland lake	Y																
Marsh lake										Y		Y					
Wet flatwoods																	
Hydric hammock													Y			Y	Y
Floodplain swamp																	
Floodplain marsh				Y	Y				Y								
Dome swamp								Y									
Depression Marshes								Y									
Baygall																	
Xeric Hammock																	
Upland Mixed Forest																	
Scrub by Flatwoods		Y															
Scrub																	
Sandhill		Y	Y			Y	Y										
Mesic Flatwoods																	

Habitat	Greenbriar	Gay feather	Deer tongue	Possumhaw	Bloodroot	Fire flag	Wild indigo	Golden aster	Pickerelweed	Reimargrass	Arrowhead	Rusty lyonia	Bladderwort	Bottlebrush threeawn	Toothache grass	Deerberry	Lizard's tail
Mesic Flatwoods																	
Sandhill							Y	Y									
Scrub												Y			Y		
Scrub by Flatwoods								Y				Y					
Upland Mixed Forest																	
Xeric Hammock				Y													
Baygall																	Y
Depression Marshes				Y	Y			Y			Y		Y				
Dome swamp					Y												Y
Floodplain marsh				Y				Y	Y		Y						Y
Floodplain swamp																	
Hydric hammock	Y	Y	Y														
Wet flatwoods																	
Marsh lake						Y		Y				Y	Y	Y			
Sandhill upland lake								Y				Y	Y				
Blackwater stream																	
Spring-run streams											Y						
Aquatic Cave																	
Sinkholes																	

Species	Mesic Flatwoods	Sandhill	Scrub	Scrub by Flatwoods	Upland Mixed Forest	Xeric Hammock	Baygall	Depression Marshes	Dome swamp	Floodplain marsh	Floodplain swamp	Hydric hammock	Wet flatwoods	Marsh lake	Sandhill upland lake	Blackwater stream	Spring-run streams	Aquatic Cave	Sinkholes
Sand pine			Y																
Rosemary			Y																
Spikerush								Y											
Floating Heart									Y										
Arum									Y										
Yelloweyed grass								Y											
Ground lichens			Y	Y															
Spanish moss									Y										
Sphagnum moss									Y										
Hog plum			Y																
Silk bay			Y										Y	Y	Y				
Spikerush													Y		Y				
Beakrush															Y				
Bulrush			Y																
Soft rush											Y								
Milk peas			Y																
Stagger bush			Y																

	Mesic Flatwoods	Sandhill	Scrub	Scrub by Flatwoods	Upland Mixed Forest	Xeric Hammock	Baygall	Depression Marshes	Dome swamp	Floodplain marsh	Floodplain swamp	Hydric hammock	Wet flatwoods	Marsh lake	Sandhill upland lake	Blackwater stream	Spring-run streams	Aquatic Cave	Sinkholes
Tarflower				Y															
Redroot									Y										
Silkbay				Y															
Garberia				Y															
Goldenrod				Y															
Pinweed				Y															
Frostweed				Y															
Pignut hickory					Y	Y													Y
Sweet gum					Y		Y				Y	Y							Y
Black gum					Y														
Maple					Y														
Red maple									Y		Y	Y							
Florida maple																			Y
Devil's walking stick					Y														
Hophornbeam																			Y
White ash																			Y

Species	Mesic Flatwoods	Sandhill	Scrub	Scrub by Flatwoods	Upland Mixed Forest	Xeric Hammock	Baygall	Depression Marshes	Dome swamp	Floodplain marsh	Floodplain swamp	Hydric hammock	Wet flatwoods	Marsh lake	Sandhill upland lake	Blackwater stream	Spring-run streams	Aquatic Cave	Sinkholes
American hornbeam					Y														
Redbud					Y														Y
Flowering dogwood					Y														
Maidencane										Y				Y					
Carolina holly					Y														
Dahoon holly							Y		Y		Y	Y							
Virginia willow							Y		Y										
American holly					Y	Y	Y												
Laurel greenbriar											Y								
Hazel alder											Y								
Hawthorn											Y								
Swamp privet							Y				Y								
Myrtle-leaved holly									Y		Y								
Pond Apple					Y														Y
Gum bumelia							Y												
Atlantic white cedar																			

	Mesic Flatwoods	Sandhill	Scrub	Scrub by Flatwoods	Upland Mixed Forest	Xeric Hammock	Baygall	Depression Marshes	Dome swamp	Floodplain marsh	Floodplain swamp	Hydric hammock	Wet Flatwoods	Marsh lake	Sandhill upland lake	Blackwater stream	Spring-run streams	Aquatic Cave	Sinkholes
Hackberry					Y							Y							
Red cedar					Y							Y							
Male-berry							Y												
Red mulberry					Y							Y							
Wild olive					Y	Y													
Redbay					Y	Y													
Laurel cherry					Y														
Black cherry					Y	Y													
Basswood					Y														
Winged elm					Y														
Florida elm					Y														
Sparkleberry					Y							Y							
Red chokeberry							Y												
Shiny lyonia													Y						
Hercules' Club					Y														
Beautyberry					Y														Y

Habitat	Partridge berry	Sarsaparilla vine	Greenbrier	Laurel greenbrier	Trilliums	Beech drops	Passion flower	Sun dews	Hat pins	Meadow Beauty	Bedstraw	Strawberry bush	Water hyssop	Spikerush	Bulrush	Bladderpod
Sinkholes			Y													
Aquatic Cave																
Spring-run streams																
Blackwater stream																
Sandhill upland lake								Y	Y	Y						
Marsh lake														Y		
Wet Flatwoods																
Hydric hammock																
Floodplain swamp																
Floodplain marsh													Y	Y	Y	
Dome swamp				Y								Y				
Depression Marshes																
Baygall																
Xeric Hammock																
Upland Mixed Forest	Y	Y	Y		Y	Y	Y				Y	Y				
Scrub by Flatwoods																
Scrub																
Sandhill																
Mesic Flatwoods																

	Cinnamon fern	Pepper vine	Common reed	Yellow jessamine	Virginia creeper	Chain fern	Netted chain fern	Venus' hair fern	Halberd fern	Maidencane	Coreopsis	Silverbell	Poison ivy	Wild grape	Partridge berry
Mesic Flatwoods															
Sandhill															
Scrub															
Scrub by Flatwoods															
Upland Mixed Forest												Y			
Xeric Hammock															
Baygall	Y					Y	Y						Y	Y	
Depression Marshes						Y	Y								
Dome swamp	Y					Y	Y			Y			Y		
Floodplain marsh			Y							Y					
Floodplain swamp															
Hydric hammock		Y		Y	Y								Y		
Wet flatwoods															
Marsh lake															
Sandhill upland lake															
Blackwater stream															
Spring-run streams															
Aquatic Cave															
Sinkholes					Y	Y	Y						Y	Y	Y

Species	Sinkholes	Aquatic Cave	Spring-run streams	Blackwater stream	Sandhill upland lake	Marsh lake	Wet flatwoods	Hydric hammock	Floodplain swamp	Floodplain marsh	Dome swamp	Depression Marshes	Baygall	Xeric Hammock	Upland Mixed Forest	Scrub by Flatwoods	Scrub	Sandhill	Mesic Flatwoods
Glasswort										Y									
Orchids											Y								
Caric sedge															Y				
Fringe tree															Y				
Horse sugar	Y														Y				
Yaupon holly															Y				
Liverwort	Y																		

ANIMALS	Mesic Flatwoods	Sandhill	Scrub	Scrub by Flatwoods	Upland Mixed Forest	Xeric Hammock	Baygall	Depression Marshes	Dome swamp	Floodplain marsh	Floodplain swamp	Hydric hammock	Wet flatwoods	Marsh lake	Sandhill upland lake	Blackwater stream	Spring-run streams	Aquatic Cave	Sinkholes
Cotton rat	Y												Y						
Wood rat					Y						Y								
Rice rat											Y								
Florida water rat														Y					
Cotton mouse	Y				Y						Y		Y						
Florida mouse			Y																
Shrew					Y														
Southern shrew							Y				Y								
Short-tailed shrew							Y				Y								
Eastern mole					Y	Y					Y								
Black bear	Y						Y				Y								
Raccoon	Y									Y									
Gray fox	Y				Y		Y				Y								
Bobcat	Y												Y						
White-tailed deer	Y				Y								Y						
Gray squirrel					Y	Y							Y						

	Mesic Flatwoods	Sandhill	Scrub	Scrub by Flatwoods	Upland Mixed Forest	Xeric Hammock	Baygall	Depression Marshes	Dome swamp	Floodplain marsh	Floodplain swamp	Hydric hammock	Wet flatwoods	Marsh lake	Sandhill upland lake	Blackwater stream	Spring-run streams	Aquatic Cave	Sinkholes
Fox squirrel		Y				Y													
Eastern flying squirrel																			
Pocket Gopher		Y																	
Marsh rabbit							Y						Y						
Cottontail rabbit																			
Southern mink							Y						Y			Y			
Spotted skunk													Y						
Striped skunk																			
Opossum							Y			Y	Y								
River otter										Y			Y						
BIRDS																			
Bald eagle													Y						
Northern harrier													Y						
Southeastern kestrel	Y																		
Red shouldered hawk											Y		Y						
Brown headed nuthatch	Y																		

	Mesic Flatwoods	Sandhill	Scrub	Scrub by Flatwoods	Upland Mixed Forest	Xeric Hammock	Baygall	Depression Marshes	Dome swamp	Floodplain marsh	Floodplain swamp	Hydric hammock	Wet flatwoods	Marsh lake	Sandhill upland lake	Blackwater stream	Spring-run streams	Aquatic Cave	Sinkholes
Bachman's sparrow	Y																		
Bobwhite		Y											Y						
Ground dove		Y	Y																
Red-headed woodpecker		Y																	
Pileated woodpecker					Y				Y		Y	Y							
Rufus-sided towhee		Y	Y																
Florida scrub jay			Y																
Blue jay						Y													
Loggerhead shrike			Y																
Acadian flycatcher											Y								
Yellow-rumped warbler			Y																
Woodcock					Y														
Barred owl					Y				Y		Y								
Screech owl						Y					Y	Y							
Wild turkey						Y													
White ibis								Y					Y						
Glossy ibis													Y						

Species	Mesic Flatwoods	Sandhill	Scrub	Scrub by Flatwoods	Upland Mixed Forest	Xeric Hammock	Baygall	Depression Marshes	Dome swamp	Floodplain marsh	Floodplain swamp	Hydric hammock	Wet flatwoods	Marsh lake	Sandhill upland lake	Blackwater stream	Spring-run streams	Aquatic Cave	Sinkholes
Wood stork								Y	Y										
Sandhill crane								Y		Y									
Wood duck															Y				
Swallow tailed kite									Y		Y								
American bittern									Y		Y								
Little bittern																			
Great-crested flycatcher									Y				Y						
Prothonotory warbler									Y				Y						
Rusty blackbird									Y		Y								
Great blue heron										Y			Y		Y				
Great egret										Y			Y		Y				
Snowy egret										Y			Y		Y				
Little blue heron										Y			Y		Y				
Tricolored heron										Y			Y		Y				
Black crowned night heron										Y					Y				
Green backed heron													Y		Y				

Species	Mesic Flatwoods	Sandhill	Scrub	Scrub by Flatwoods	Upland Mixed Forest	Xeric Hammock	Baygall	Depression Marshes	Dome swamp	Floodplain marsh	Floodplain swamp	Hydric hammock	Wet flatwoods	Marsh lake	Sandhill upland lake	Blackwater stream	Spring-run streams	Aquatic Cave	Sinkholes
Yellow crowned night heron										Y	Y				Y				
Limpkin													Y						
Chimney swift											Y								
King rail													Y						
Virginia rail													Y						
Carolina wren											Y								
Long-billed marsh wren																			
White-eyed vireo											Y		Y						
Red-eyed vireo											Y								
Pine warbler	Y																		
Parula warbler											Y								
Hooded warbler											Y								
Swainson's warbler											Y								
Cardinal											Y								
Towhee											Y								
Yellowthroat													Y						

Species	Sinkholes	Aquatic Cave	Spring-run streams	Blackwater stream	Sandhill upland lake	Marsh lake	Wet flatwoods	Hydric hammock	Floodplain swamp	Floodplain marsh	Dome swamp	Depression Marshes	Baygall	Xeric Hammock	Upland Mixed Forest	Scrub by Flatwoods	Scrub	Sandhill	Mesic Flatwoods
Red winged blackbird							Y												
Boat-tailed grackle							Y												
FISH																			
River longnose gar				Y															
Gizzard shad				Y															
Threadfin shad				Y															
Redfin pickerel				Y															
Chain pickerel				Y															
Ironcolor shiner				Y															
Ohoopee shiner				Y															
Weed shiner				Y															
Blacktail shiner				Y															
Chubsucker				Y															
Channel catfish				Y															
Banded topminnow				Y															
Pygmy killifish				Y															

Species	Mesic Flatwoods	Sandhill	Scrub	Scrub by Flatwoods	Upland Mixed Forest	Xeric Hammock	Baygall	Depression Marshes	Dome swamp	Floodplain marsh	Floodplain swamp	Hydric hammock	Wet flatwoods	Marsh lake	Sandhill upland lake	Blackwater stream	Spring-run streams	Aquatic Cave	Sinkholes
Mosquitofish																Y			
Mud sunfish																Y			
Banded sunfish																Y			
Redbreast sunfish																Y			
Dollar sunfish																Y			
Stumpknocker																Y			
Black crappie																Y			
Spotted bass																Y			
Darters																Y			

OTHER CREATURES	Mesic Flatwoods	Sandhill	Scrub	Scrub by Flatwoods	Upland Mixed Forest	Xeric Hammock	Baygall	Depression Marshes	Dome swamp	Floodplain marsh	Floodplain swamp	Hydric hammock	Wet flatwoods	Marsh lake	Sandhill upland lake	Blackwater stream	Spring-run streams	Aquatic Cave	Sinkholes
Alligator									Y	Y				Y		Y	Y		
Oak toad	Y																		
Southern toad			Y										Y						
Bullfrog														Y					
River frog	Y															Y			
Little grass frog	Y										Y								
Narrowmouth toad											Y								
Cope's gray treefrog					Y						Y								
Pig frog									Y										
Leopard frog						Y		Y		Y	Y			Y					
Gopher frog		Y						Y		Y			Y	Y	Y				
Cricket frog								Y		Y	Y								
Bronze frog					Y									Y					
Eastern spadefoot toad		Y						Y											
Little grass frog								Y	Y										
Southern cricket frog									Y										

Guide to the Wekiva River Basin State Parks   173

	Mesic Flatwoods	Sandhill	Scrub	Scrub by Flatwoods	Upland Mixed Forest	Xeric Hammock	Baygall	Depression Marshes	Dome swamp	Floodplain marsh	Floodplain swamp	Hydric hammock	Wet flatwoods	Marsh lake	Sandhill upland lake	Blackwater stream	Spring-run streams	Aquatic Cave	Sinkholes
Southern chorus frog								Y					Y						
Ornate chorus frog								Y											
Oak toad								Y	Y										
Barking treefrog		Y				Y		Y											
Green Treefrog									Y		Y								
Gray treefrog														Y					
Pinewoods treefrog								Y											
Bird-voiced tree frog											Y								
Squirrel treefrog								Y	Y		Y								
Black Racer	Y					Y							Y						
Cottonmouth																			
Gray rat snake					Y														
Rough green snake					Y														
Coral snake					Y	Y													
Red rat snake	Y																		
Yellow rat snake													Y						
Mud snake											Y								

Snake	Mesic Flatwoods	Sandhill	Scrub	Scrub by Flatwoods	Upland Mixed Forest	Xeric Hammock	Baygall	Depression Marshes	Dome swamp	Floodplain marsh	Floodplain swamp	Hydric hammock	Wet flatwoods	Marsh lake	Sandhill upland lake	Blackwater stream	Spring-run streams	Aquatic Cave	Sinkholes
Rainbow snake											Y						Y		
Hognose snake						Y													
Red-bellied snake					Y														
Red belly water snake						Y					Y					Y	Y		
Crowned snake																			
Brown water snake											Y					Y	Y		
Green water snake														Y					
Black swamp snake														Y					
Indigo snake		Y																	
Coachwhip snake		Y																	
Pine snake		Y																	
Eastern mud snake									Y	Y									
Banded water snake										Y				Y					
Striped swamp snake										Y				Y					
Short-tailed snake		Y																	
Crowned snake		Y																	
Eastern diamondback rattlesnake		Y																	

Habitat occurrence table (Y = species occurs in habitat)

Species	Mesic Flatwoods	Sandhill	Scrub	Scrub by Flatwoods	Upland Mixed Forest	Xeric Hammock	Baygall	Depression Marshes	Dome swamp	Floodplain marsh	Floodplain swamp	Hydric hammock	Wet Flatwoods	Marsh lake	Sandhill upland lake	Blackwater stream	Spring-run streams	Aquatic Cave	Sinkholes
Pygmy rattlesnake		Y											Y						
Gopher tortoise						Y													
Box turtle					Y														
Snapping turtle									Y							Y			
Striped mud turtle									Y										
Mud turtle									Y		Y								
River cooter																Y			
Florida cooter																Y			
Stinkpot												Y				Y			
Tiger salamander		Y						Y											
Slimy salamander					Y		Y												
Mole salamander									Y		Y								
Two-lined salamander									Y		Y								
Rusty mud salamander											Y								
Three-lined salamander											Y								
Dwarf salamander								Y	Y		Y								
Marbled salamander											Y								

	Mesic Flatwoods	Sandhill	Scrub	Scrub by Flatwoods	Upland Mixed Forest	Xeric Hammock	Baygall	Depression Marshes	Dome swamp	Floodplain marsh	Floodplain swamp	Hydric hammock	Wet flatwoods	Marsh lake	Sandhill upland lake	Blackwater stream	Spring-run streans	Aquatic Cave	Sinkholes
Southern dusky salamander							Y				Y								
Southern mud salamander							Y												
Flatwoods salamander								Y	Y										
Blind cave salamander																		Y	
Worm lizard		Y				Y													
Fence lizard		Y				Y													
Mole skink		Y																	
Eastern glass lizard					Y														
Blue-tailed mole skink			Y																
Broadhead skink												Y							
Southeastern five-lined skink												Y							
Broadhead skink					Y														
Ground skink					Y														
Green anole			Y		Y														
Sand skink			Y																
Red widow spider			Y												Y				
Striped newt								Y											

Species	Sinkholes	Aquatic Cave	Spring-run streams	Blackwater stream	Sandhill upland lake	Marsh lake	Wet flatwoods	Hydric hammock	Floodplain swamp	Floodplain marsh	Dome swamp	Depression Marshes	Baygall	Xeric Hammock	Upland Mixed Forest	Scrub by Flatwoods	Scrub	Sandhill	Mesic Flatwoods
Scrub wolf spider																	Y		
Six-lined racerunner																	Y		
Coachwhip snake																	Y		
Amphiuma						Y			Y										
Alabama waterdog				Y					Y										
Lesser siren						Y													
Greater siren						Y													
Stonefly			Y																
Mayfly			Y																
Caddisfly			Y																
Orlando cave crayfish		Y																	
Blind cave crayfish		Y																	
Cave shrimp		Y																	
Cave snail		Y																	

Notes

Notes

Notes

Notes

Notes

Notes